M. Payoly

JESUS´ YEARS
IN INDIA

FACTS REVEALING THE TRUTH

Copyright: © 2018 M. Payoly

Publisher: tredition GmbH, Hamburg

978-3-7469-5460-8 (Paperback)
978-3-7469-5461-5 (Hardcover)
978-3-7469-5462-2 (e-Book)

Bibliographic Information of the German National Library:
The German National Library has listed this publication in the "Deutsche Nationalbibliografie"; you can access detailed information through the internet at http://dnb.d-nb.de

The author

M. Payoly was born in Kerala State, India.

This book is dedicated
to my mother

Content

To whatever religious creed a man may belong and whatever may be his position in society, if he purely cultivates this ruling principle naturally implanted in his heart, he is sure to be on the right path, to save himself from wandering in this creation of Darkness, Maya.

Swami Sri Yukteswar

Life is always unsafe and unstable like a drop of water on a lotus leaf. The company of a divine personage, even for a moment, can save and redeem us.

Sri Shankaracharya

FOREWORD

The purpose of this book is to reveal and justify the real Jesus Christ. For the true believers and admirers of Jesus Christ, it is hardly possible to believe some of the dogmas established by the Roman Church on Christianity over 1900 years. These dogmas cannot be explained logically, and if one thinks about them and questions a Christian priest, the answers are suffocating with long explanations. And eventually one will hear: *"the Christian dogmas are beyond human logic"*.

One who is born in India, a land of many religions, is lucky because he gets exposed to Hinduism, Islam, Buddhism, Jainism and Christianity. All the religions of the world find followers in India. This cosmopolitanism is the most attractive cornerstone for an Indian child to build his life on. His friends in the neighborhood and in the school, with whom he plays, are from families practising different religions. This helps him to pick up knowledge of other religions subconsciously right from childhood by attending various festivals, where he is a curious participant. Irrespective of the religion of his birth, he grows up with a ready acquaintance of prominent names in various religions such as Krishna and Arjuna, Rama, Lakshmana and Sita, the Mahabharata and Ramayana, the Buddha, Jesus Christ, Muhammad and Shankaracharya. Indeed, the Indian child acquires this precious spiritual capital in his early childhood. By the time he grows into an adult, the differences of the various religions are neither strange nor hostile to him.

I was born in a Thomas Christian family in Kerala, India. It was a privilege to be born in Kerala (advertised as God's Own Country) where Shankaracharya (788-820) and Narayana Guru (1855-1928), the redeemers of Hinduism, were born. It is accepted among the philosophers in the world that Shankaracharya was the most logical thinker ever born. Shankaracharya has said:

Do not blindly believe and follow my words. What I said and wrote is what I really experienced as a human being. You and I are equal. If you really follow what I said, you would experience what I experienced. If you really tried and not achieved what I said, throw it away and do not follow me.

He tells us clearly to believe in only that which our logical thinking can accept and not follow him blindly.

Prophets proclaimed many years before Jesus` birth that a Messiah would be born and forecast where He would be born. We know about His childhood from the Holy Bible. However, there is a vacuum in the New Testament about Jesus` life between the ages of 13 and 29. It is illogical to believe that this pious young man spent all these years working as a carpenter, helping His father Joseph in Palestine, His existence entirely unknown to the world. But if there are ample evidences that Jesus was in India during that period, learning and visiting Hindu temples and Buddhist monasteries, and preaching His *new faith* to the common people, why can`t this be acknowledged?

There are three special dogmas in the Roman Church which defy logic, namely, the resurrection of Jesus Christ after crucifixion, the bodily ascension of Jesus Christ and the bodily ascension of His mother Mary to heaven.

There is an eternal truth: *if one is born on earth, he shall die on earth.*

In the case of Jesus and Mary, the Church makes an exception, namely that they *ascended bodily* into heaven. This is beyond logic.

But there are clear evidences in India and Kashmir that Jesus and Mary arrived in Taxila, capital of the Parthian Empire, in AD 49, after the ordeal on the cross.

8

Why did the Roman Church hide that information from the Christian believers all these centuries?

One can assume that the Church fathers wanted to save Jesus from the Romans who doubted His death on the cross and had, therefore, sent Him to a far off land outside the Roman Empire. If that were the case, the question arises: why didn't the Church correct the record after the decline of the Roman Empire?

The Church didn`t.

In order to rectify a lie, one has to lie again and again; but a lie always remains a lie and it can never be equal to the truth.

In 1974 I read an interesting article in a German weekly *Stern* written by two German journalists, Mr Claus Liedtke and Mr Jay Ullal. They had visited Kashmir and talked with the famous archaeologist Prof. Fida Hassnain about the life of Jesus in Kashmir after the crucifixion. Professor Hassnain, a Kashmiri Muslim and a neutral researcher about Jesus of long standing, gave them all the information he had gathered about Jesus in India, Kashmir and Tibet.

Professor Hassnain had learnt that Jesus had come to India as a 13-year-old and stayed in Hindu temples learning Yoga, the Vedas and other Hindu scriptures. He also visited Buddhist temples and monasteries in India, Nepal and Tibet and spent many years learning Buddhist scriptures. He preached His *new faith* to the common people in market places and visited many places in India. When He was about 29 years old, He returned to Palestine to fulfil His *mission*. After the crucifixion, Jesus returned to India and reached Taxila, capital of Parthian Empire, in AD 49. Later He moved to Kashmir and died in Kashmir at the age of 117.

For Professor Hassnain there was a missing link: how was and who saved Jesus after the crucifixion? But now that missing link has been found and the truth is there for everybody who is interested in Jesus` life.

Every Indian child comes in contact with the Mahabharata and Ramayana (Indian epics) from primary school onwards without considering his religion. It is a fact that there are many religions in India, especially minority religions like Islam, Christianity, Sikhism and Jainism. But there is one common factor: irrespective of the minority religion one belongs to India, everyone, with small exceptions, had Hindu ancestry. Not even one per cent of the Christians and Muslims in India would claim that their ancestors hailed from either Rome or Arabia. Only the religions were foreign. And persons like me, born in a Syrian Christian family in Kerala, are really proud of the ancestry. Because of the plurality prevailing in India, the religious truths one gets from schools, from friends and from the holy books are so rich.

As far as I know, there is no religion in the world which is as tolerant as Hinduism. It is a fact. All Christians and Muslims of Kerala know from their own history how the Hindu kings of Kerala welcomed the new religious people, helped them to build their churches and mosques and gave them land for farming and business. There was no discrimination and they did not consider them as foreigners - only the religions were foreign.

Swami Vivekananda said:

"I am proud to belong to a religion which has taught the world both tolerance and universal acceptance. We believe not only in universal toleration, but we accept all religions as true. I am proud to belong to a nation which has sheltered the persecuted and the refugees of all religions and all nations of the earth."[1]

India was a country which was conquered by Alexander the Great from Greece and the Moguls from Central Asia. Because of the universal

---

[1] Swami Vivekananda: speech at the World Parliament of Religions in Chicago, September 27, 1893.

10

tolerance that existed in Hinduism, India could absorb the new cultures without offending her indigenous identity.

"It is the unique nature of Hinduism to accept and absorb new ideas and appreciate them. Hinduism has an open mind, respects all other faiths and sentiments and embraces them."[2]

Since centuries the Hindus in India have not been against other religions. They were spiritual and their aim of life on earth was to attain God. According to Hindu tenets, religion was *only a way* to attain God and nothing more. Quoting from Swami Vivekananda's famous speech in Chicago:

"I will quote to you, brethren, a few lines from a hymn which I remember to have repeated from my earliest childhood, which is everyday repeated by millions of human beings: "As the different streams having their sources in different places all mingle their water in the sea so, O Lord, lie different paths which men take through different tendencies, various though they appear, crooked or straight, all lead to Thee."[3]

If there are many religions, one can choose one that suits him and try to attain God. Swami Vivekananda went further: *Each person should have a religion suitable for him.* How could then a true Hindu become a religious fanatic?

The social history of India underwent changes after Vivekananda. There came a new religion in the name of politics. The politicians misused the feelings of the normal man and made many Indians religious fanatics. They used religion as a weapon to garner votes and the consequence was the massacres of innocent minorities as it happened even as recently as in 2002 in the State of Gujarat. The perpetrators were not at all *real* Hindus. They were people who respected neither Hinduism nor the age-old social

---

[2] Bharat, Sandy: *Christ Across the Ganges*, O Books, UK 2007, Appendices, p. 158.
[3] Swami Vivekananda: op.cit.

harmony that prevailed in Indian society. At the same time, one thing was astonishing, worth appreciation and outstanding: the hard opposition those fanatics encountered also came from the Hindus. They were morally courageous Hindu police officers and Hindu women working in social fields who went to court and told the truth and protected the minorities. People like them are the *true Hindus* of modern India who have been brought up in real Hindu families upholding and respecting the principles of Hinduism.

Jesus was an Indian because He spent most of His life in India. But many of His followers did not know about the real life of Jesus because the Roman Church had manipulated the truth and brought up *dogmas* which were beyond human logic.

What I have tried here is to present the real life of Jesus, re-connecting the missing links. If one is a follower or admirer of Jesus, one has the opportunity to go through the referenced books given in each chapter and enlighten his knowledge and belief and understand the *real* Jesus.

7th June, 2018

Chapter 1

Who is Jesus?

The historical life of Jesus is simple to understand. But his followers have made it purposely so complicated, and sometimes beyond reason, it has become so difficult for a common man to understand Him. So many are the dogmas and mysteries. Either one has to believe blindly those dogmas without reason until one dies as an obedient and God-fearing Christian, never learning what really Jesus wanted, or one has to leave the Church. Unfortunately, until very recently, the Roman Church, with its undisputed clout, would not let its critics go in peace and hounded them to their graves, making their life miserable.

Many horrible deeds were done in the name of Jesus, the pious Son of God and friend of the poor. What He came for, what He taught mankind and where He was between the ages of 13 and 29 were never mentioned in the history of the Church of Rome.

He taught tolerance to others, but His followers never tolerated. He taught to love one another, but His followers hated those who did not believe in the Church. He asked not to kill, even animals, but his followers killed thousands of human beings in His name. He asked for freedom for all, but the countries in Europe, influenced by the Christian Church, colonized other continents and destroyed thriving civilizations and cultures and looted their wealth and put innocent people under the yoke of foreign rule, denying them their freedom for hundreds of years. He taught that '*The Kingdom of God is within you*' and that one has to find God '*while one lives on earth*', but His followers projected a God of aggressive and unsympathetic mien, attainable only after death and created heaven and hell. He came to redeem the poor, break their chains of slavery and save them from ignorance, but His followers put many under chains and made them slaves, scattering their families across continents and selling them as slaves. He sent His beloved disciple Thomas to Kerala in AD 52 to teach His *new faith*, but the Church of Rome, through the Portuguese colonial power, manipulated their original belief in Jesus Christ, their old customs and even terrorized His believers and burned their original books and even imposed *inquisition* on them.

The Church of Rome manipulated and rewrote His words and even sent Him and His mother *bodily* to heaven, which is contrary to natural law made by God.

His followers in Europe preached and taught in His name in different continents upholding and supporting the political interests of their kings and the Pope. They were fanatical and powerful. They had only one doctrine: *"Ours is the BEST religion; all other religions that existed in the continents since centuries were not at all to attain God."* They monopolized not only the *one God*, but also the *way* to attain Him. For them all other ways to attain Him were wrong and worthless.

They did this for hundreds of years in the name of Jesus, the pious, the merciful, the redeemer, the friend of the unprivileged.

Jesus was saved after the crucifixion and He secretly left Palestine for Kashmir in order to avoid Roman punishment once again. He passed through Syria, Persia, Afghanistan and reached Taxila, the capital of the Parthian Kingdom. The Roman Church knew the truth, but not its followers.

Jesus became a 'prisoner' of the Church from about AD 36. The Church suffocated Him, did not allow Him to speak the truth. Millions of people *blindly* followed and believed the untruths and dogmas up to their graves. If anybody tried to find the truth about Jesus in Europe, the powerful Roman Church hounded them and made their life very difficult. The Roman Church was powerful and would spread its net worldwide in order to render the truth seeker *silent.* Any document found anywhere in the world about the real Jesus was burned or bought off and suppressed at the source. The Church had no scruples about the means it adopted in order to suppress the truth.

They did this in the name of Jesus, the Son of God, who was born and died a poor in order to redeem humanity. His words are *universal and valid for all people to free the soul within* and He showed the way to attain God during one's *life on earth.* But the Roman Church *lost the way* after about AD 250.

The Church of Rome, His official follower, put Him *in prison* after His crucifixion in AD 36.

The time has come to free Him from the chains of lies, false dogmas and superstitions in order to tell mankind the TRUTH about the real Jesus, His life, His work and His death and ultimately to redeem the Christian Church. Jesus' words are *universal and are for all people* on earth. The Roman Church has no right or moral authority to keep the real life of Jesus a secret from His followers and the world.

Chapter 2

What was the Purpose of Jesus' Birth?

It was prophesied in various religious books that God would send His son or a prophet to earth whenever there was a suppression of His folk or He would assign prophets to do a particular work. There had been many such manifestations in many religions, noticed or unnoticed, and some of the more important among them have been of Moses in Egypt, the Buddha in India, Jesus in Palestine, Muhammad in Arabia and Shankaracharya in India. When a society degenerated, God sent His representative to redeem the society and uplift them by showing a way and upholding moral principles. The new *teacher* would teach universal truths defining *each truth, which is one and indivisible.* Though the epochs were different, the truths they preached were simple and universal and understandable for the common man.

The common man in the modern world, Christian or non-Christian, did not know the real life of Jesus. They knew only a part of it.

Some mighty persons or powerful organizations might manipulate the *truth* for some time, perhaps several years; but one day it would come out, crushing all lies, dogmas and myths.

As Prof. Max Mueller said:

"Truth is truth, whether it is accepted now or in millions of years. Truth is in no hurry, at least it always seemed to me so."[1]

The birth of Jesus was not only expected long before He was born, but there were also prophesies about where He would be born and how His

---

[1] Prof. Mueller, Max: *My Autobiography*, Longmans, Green, And Co., London, 1901, Chapter IX, p. 301.

life would be. As He was born, according to the Bible, there came three kings from the East to worship the Son of God whom they had awaited for so long. But the same Bible gives no details about what He did and where He was between the ages of 13 and 29 years.

Why did the Bible provide no detailed information about the life of Jesus during that period? It is illogical to think that He stayed with His family for so long in silence assisting His father Joseph.

He was born in a stable and the animals were the witnesses. He was born as the poorest among the poor.

The young and pious Mary was selected by God as His mother and He was born even as she was a virgin. Some people would oppose that theory of Immaculate Conception from a modern biological viewpoint, but one could come across many such stories in Buddhist and Hindu Scriptures as well as stories of famous Yogis of India, which serve to show that people had been aware of stories of divine births. But Jesus said it Himself, in a conversation in His later years in a foreign country, that He was *"born of a virgin"*.

His mother was Mary, the virgin, and His adoptive father was Joseph, the carpenter. We know from the Bible that Joseph was privy to the secret and purpose of the birth of Jesus and that Jesus spent His childhood with them in harmony.

According to other documents, Mary had other children from Joseph and it is natural and logical. Joseph was a widower und it is natural to think that he had children in his first marriage. Famous among the children in the family were Jesus` elder brother James (called *James the just)* and Thomas. The former became the first Bishop of Palestine after Jesus' crucifixion. James contradicted many things St. Paul had advocated after the crucifixion of Jesus. James died a martyr in the hands of the Romans.

Is the New Testament a truthful documentation of what Jesus said and preached? Or have they been manipulated by Church Fathers under the influence of Roman Emperors who accepted Christianity in later years, such as Constantine and Justinian? It is history that the Bible was burned several times and that new texts were created to suit the interests of the rulers and the hierarchy in the Christian Church.

They added new dogmas about Jesus' Resurrection from the dead and Ascension into heaven, which the obedient and God-fearing Christians believed until now.

Many of the texts that we read in the Bible are not the original texts.

The Jews were the chosen folk. God had given them all, but they misused His words. They became prisoners in Egypt, where they lived as slaves for many years. As they prayed and asked God to save them from captivity in Egypt, the merciful Father sent Moses to save them. Many years later, they again forgot His words and did all things that they were not supposed to do. God again punished His folk.

According to Jewish history, there were *twelve tribes* of Jews in Palestine. By the time Jesus was born, only two tribes remained in Palestine and the rest ten had been captured and brought to Persia who later migrated to the Parthian Empire, including Afghanistan, Kashmir, Ladakh and Nepal. Those ten tribes were known in Church history as the *"lost sheep of Israel or Bani Israel"*.

Jesus said, *"I am not sent but unto the lost sheep of the house of Israel"* (Matthew 15:25).

Until he was about 13 years old, Jesus stayed with His parents in Palestine. Then He left Palestine for India, studied Hindu scriptures and Yoga and visited Hindu temples and Buddhist monasteries and preached to the common people about His *new faith*. He vehemently opposed the *caste*

19

system and *animal slaughter* practised in Hindu society. He studied, toured and preached throughout India for 16 years and travelled to Egypt and stayed two years in the desert monastery of the *Brotherhood.* Then He returned to Palestine to fulfil His mission. He was about 31 years old.

As a preacher He stayed again some years in Palestine with the *two tribes*. He was crucified but rescued from the cross. He spent the rest of His life with *the lost tribes* in Kashmir in fulfilment of His mission on earth.

Chapter 3

The History of the Ten Tribes

Jacob had twelve sons from his wives and concubines and the twelve tribes were the descendants of each son and they were known in history as *the Children of Israel,* and in the East as *Bani Israel.* After the death of Solomon, the Jews of Palestine were divided into two groups. Two tribes of Jews, Judah and Benjamin, lived in Jerusalem and the remaining ten formed the Kingdom of Israel with Samaria as their capital. The two groups were not always on friendly terms and sometimes fought each other.

They were reunited under King David around BC 970 and Palestine became a prosperous country. But by BC 926 the kingdom collapsed again forming two states namely Israel and Judah and later they fought each other.

For the first time the Assyrians attacked Samaria in BC 740 and took many Jews as prisoners.

"In the year before Christ 721, Salmanazar, king of Assyria, took the city after three years, and carried away ten tribes of Israel (or most of them *) into captivity, and so put an end to that kingdom after it had stood 254 years divided from that of Judah."*[1]

The captives were taken to Assyria, Mesopotamia and Media.

When Nebuchadnezzar became the ruler of Babylon and Media, he conquered the Kingdom of Judah (BC 597) and took a considerable part of the Jews belonging to the two tribes to Babylon. The next deportation

---

[1] Flavius Josephus

on a large scale followed in the year BC 587. And finally he brought Jerusalem under control and destroyed the city, seized their wealth and transported the people to Babylon.

The third and last deportation was in BC 582, by which event all the Jews had been brought to Babylon.

The Jews under captivity in Babylon evolved and adopted the Aramaic script.

In the year BC 538 Cyrus the Great, King of Persia, captured Babylon and freed the Jews and allowed them to return to *Yehud Province* and rebuild the Temple. Two tribes, Judah and Benjamin, returned to Jerusalem; but most of the ten tribes remained in Babylon. During their captivity, many of the Jews had married native women and had children. Those who left for Jerusalem left their wives and children behind in Babylon and the others (the ten tribes) moved to Persia.

Cyrus' successor, Darius Hystapis, extended the boundaries of the Persian Empire to Greece in the west, India in the east and Afghanistan in the north.

God scattered them *"among all the nations whom they knew not. Thus the land was desolate after them, that no man passed through nor returned".*[2]

They moved from Persia to Afghanistan, to Kashmir and the northern parts of India and later to southern India. They settled in new countries, never to return to Jerusalem, but took care to keep their identity and religious customs under their respective tribes.

It is a fact that, *"the Jewish people are a very distinctive people. They have developed an identity as a group, with related physical features, common traditions, language and religion, that has lasted longer than any*

---

[2] Zecharih

other group in history, and this despite the fact that, more than any other people, they have been persecuted and enslaved. The Jews have been stateless for some 1900 years".[3]

Many early foreign travelers, even Christian priests who visited Afghanistan and Kashmir, had written that the people living there were not of Asian origin and their features were similar to that of the Jews.

Many of their names, physical features, customs and burial ceremonies, too, were Jewish.

They also named places in Kashmir and Afghanistan after place names in Syria and Palestine.

There is no clear evidence in the Middle East as to where Moses died and was buried and it is still a mystery, whereas *"There is lot of evidence that he came to Cashmere in the last days".[4]*

There are plenty of records to show that during the time of Soloman there had been contacts with India and particularly with Kashmir. *"Cashmere is still known among the local Muslim population as Bagh-i- Suleiman, the 'Garden of Solomon', and on a mountain that overlooks the city of Srinagar there stands a small temple called Takht-i-Suleiman, 'the Throne of Solomon'."[5]*

So Kashmir was a beloved and chosen place for the Jewish people.

According to Kashmir history, Khalid-ibn-al-Walid converted them to Islam in AD 633.

Even the Kashmiri Pandits (Brahmins) and Kashmiri Muslims kept many

---

[3] Hassnain, Prof. Fida: *A Search for the Historical Jesus*, Gateway Books, UK 1994, Chapter 1, p.3

[4] ibid, Chapter 1, p. 5

[5] Kersten, Holger: *Jesus Lived in India*, Penguin Books, India, 2001, Chapter 3, p. 49

common customs. Many historians believe that the present day Kashmiri Pandits were descendants of *Bani Israel* who adopted Hinduism.

Did the Church know about the early life of Israelites, *the lost sheep*, living in Asia?

"There are evidences that the followers of Bani Israel lived in Nagaland, Bombay (Mumbai), Tamil Nadu (Madras), Mangalore, and Kozhikode (Calicut), Cochin, Palayur and Quilon in Kerala. The first people converted to Christianity by Apostle Thomas at Palayur, north of Cochin, in AD 52 were Jews."[6]

---

[6] Benhur, Abraham : *The Jewish Background of Indian Christians*, Jeevanist Books, Calicut, 2011

Chapter 4

The Life of Jesus Between 13 and 29 Years

This is a very controversial part in the life of Jesus. His birth was predicted centuries ago and the people waited for the *Messiah*. The only official information we have about His birth is from the Bible written by Matthew, Luke, Mark and John before AD 90, but it is known that their accounts were modified after the 1st century. Mark and Luke were not Apostles, but companions of St. Peter and St. Paul, respectively. Even the Biblical description about Jesus` adulthood and life as a grown up man are not very clear. The Bible, as we have it today, gives preponderant space to Jesus' last three years as a preacher in Palestine and the crucifixion.

One important information we have in the Bible about His childhood is that His parents searched for Him and found Him in discussion with the high priests in the Temple of Jerusalem. Answering his mother, Jesus says,

"Why do you seek me? Don't you know that I must be careful in the matter regarding my Father?" (Luke 2:49)

It is astonishing and unacceptable for a normal Christian the one sentence description given in the Bible about His life between 13 and 29 years:

"And Jesus kept increasing in wisdom and stature, and in favor with God and men." (Luke 2:52)

It is difficult for a true believer in Jesus Christ to accept this bare version given in the Bible and the doctrines followed by the Church since centuries because it does not agree with logical thinking. Naturally, he will search for other documents or evidence existing elsewhere.

When a true believer in Jesus makes a research in the history of the Christian Church from its humble beginning in the 1st century until now, he has two possibilities:

- Either he loses his faith in Christianity,

- Or he remains a true believer in Jesus Christ, rejecting several of the Church's teachings that led to the perpetration of untold cruelties on mankind in Europe and other continents for centuries in the name of Jesus Christ.

What the Church did down centuries was the opposite of what Jesus had taught. The Church sided with emperors, kings, landlords and brutal dictators until the middle of the 20th century in order to keep their power and material comforts. Some of the early Popes and bishops wielded more power than kings and many of them have been declared saints. The brutal practice of *Inquisition,* exercised in Europe against opponents and believers who challenged the authorities, was taken even to India in order to suppress the native Thomas Christians of Kerala who rebelled against imposition of Portuguese colonial rule over the Church with Roman concurrence. The man who *begged* for permission from the Portuguese King John III, which was endorsed by the Pope, to introduce *Inquisition* in Goa was none other than the first Jesuit missionary Francis Xavier, one of the great saints and thinkers in the Roman Catholic Church.

"The Holy Office of the Inquisition was established in India at the instigation of the first Jesuit Missionary. In a letter dated 10th November 1545, St. Francis Xavier begged John III of Portugal to grant this favour on the plea that `the Jewish wickedness` spread daily in this Indian dominions. The proposal commended itself to the royal mind, and the Inquisition was at length set up in 1560 at Goa, where for more than 250 years it was maintained in terrible severity. All the Inquisitors were nominated by the King of Portugal and confirmed by the Pope, from whom they received their bulls. .... The property of prisoners was almost invariably confiscated, and became, in whole or in part, the property of the Holy Office".[1]

---

[1] Milne Rae, George : *The Syrian Church in India*, Cornell University `s print collection, USA, Chapter XIV, pp.198-199

Those atrocities were perpetrated on the Thomas Christians of Kerala who had been the followers of Saint Thomas since AD 52. The Portuguese burned the Bible the Kerala Christians had been following since Saint Thomas and replaced it with the new manipulated Bible approved by Rome. The Christian priests of Kerala, who had not practised celibacy, were prohibited from officiating in mass. The Thomas Christians had been under the Patriarch of Syria, and not the Pope, ever since the advent of the Church in Kerala.

Many of the practices of the Roman Church in the past were not only brutal and inhuman but also the opposite of what Jesus had preached.

Therefore, a true believer in Jesus has the right to find out the truth about Jesus` whereabouts between the ages of 13 and 29 years and also His life after the crucifixion.

But we don't need to wait for millions of years for the truth to emerge as Max Mueller feared.

Some important evidences about Jesus` adult life are available in various documents as detailed below:

1. Early Buddhist Documents

Gautama Buddha was born about 563 years before Jesus. In his last years, the Buddha predicted that another *Buddha* would be born on earth when his own teachings undergo degeneration. He named him *Methyya* and even spoke about his light complexion and that he would be born in a foreign country.

According to Max Muller *Methyya* means Messiah.

The Buddha was an Indian with dark complexion whereas Jesus born in Palestine had light complexion.

The Buddhists also called Jesus as Saint Issa.

2. *"The Unknown life of Jesus Christ"* **written by Nicolas Notovitch**

This book published in the western world details seminal research into Jesus' life between 13 and 29 years.

Nicolas Notovitch was a Russian journalist interested in the people and archaeology of India. After the Russo-Turkish war in 1877-78, he undertook many travels in the East. He had enough money and courage to take adventurous trips. He came to India through Afghanistan and visited Lahore and Rawalpindi and was interested in Kashmir. His original plan was to visit Kashmir and Ladakh and then return to Russia through eastern Turkey and Karakoram. On the way, he visited the Buddhist Monastery at Mulbekh. There he met the chief lama in the convent and had a good conversation. The lama told him:

"The only error of the Christians is that after adopting the great doctrine of Buddha, they, at the very outset, completely separated themselves from him and created another Dalai-Lama; while ours alone has received the divine favor of seeing the majesty of Buddha face to face, and the power of serving as intermediary between heaven and earth."

They spoke about Issa (Jesus) and the lama said again:

"Issa is a great prophet, one of the first after the twenty-two Buddhas; he is greater than any of the Dalai – Lama, for he constitutes a part of the spirituality of the Lord. It is he who has instructed you, who has

brought back frivolous souls to God, who has rendered you worthy of the blessings of the creator, who has endowed each creature with the knowledge of good and evil. His name and his deeds have been recorded in our sacred writings, and, whilst reading of his great existence spent in the midst of erring people, we weep over the horrible sin of the pagans, who assassinated him and put him to the most cruel tortures." [2]

During the conversation, Notovitch came to know about the existence of old parchment records about Issa in the archives of the monastery in Lhasa, capital of Tibet. The lama told him that copies of the parchments were also available in other Buddhist monasteries. He visited some other monasteries and finally reached the famous Hemis monastery at Leh in Ladakh in 1887.

He stayed there for some days as a guest during the famous *Padma sambhava* festival time. Finally he got the opportunity to meet the chief lama and they talked for long about both Buddhism and Christianity. Notovitch asked the lama about the Jesus` parchments in the monastery. The lama answered that the monastery possessed one roll about Jesus written in the Tibetan language. The lama told him that Jesus was the incarnation of the Buddha and was born in Israel. He also said:

"When the sacred child had attained a certain age, he was taken to India, where, until he attained manhood, he studied the laws of the Great Buddha who resides eternally in heaven". [3]

The lama informed him that he needed time to search for and find the scrolls about Jesus.

[2] Notovitch, Nicolas : *The Unknown Life of Jesus Christ*, Tree of Life Publications Joshua Tree, California, 1996, pp. 20-21
[3] ibid., p. 31

"Should you ever again visit our gompa, however, I will show them to you with pleasure".[4]

Notovitch wanted to return to Kashmir first and come back again to see the scrolls.

He left the convent and some days later fell down from his horse and broke his leg. As the Hemis Monastery was the nearest place where he could get proper help, he returned to the monastery and stayed there for many days under treatment. One day the chief lama called him to his room and showed him the scrolls containing the life of Jesus. It was written in the Tibetan language and Notovitch was allowed to transcribe it with the help of a translator and he wrote it down in his notebook.

It described the birth of Issa, His arrival as a young man in Sind, His stay in the Jagannath Temple in Puri and visits to other places in India to study Hindu and Buddhist texts, His eventual return to Palestine and the crucifixion. The text was written after the crucifixion. Jesus was well known among the Buddhist lamas as he visited India as a young man. He learned in the Buddhist monasteries. When the lamas later heard about the crucifixion of the pious Jesus from Indian and other merchants coming from Palestine, they collected all evidences of Jesus` life they had and chronicled them on parchments.

The parchments did not record the life of Jesus in a chronological order, according to Notovich, which he did.

The reason why Jesus left His family in Palestine when He was thirteen was:

> *"When Issa had attained the age of thirteen, when an Israelite should take a wife, The house in which his parents dwelt and earned their livelihood in modest*

---

[4] ibid., p. 31

labour, became a meeting place for the rich and noble, who desired to gain for a son - in- law the young Issa, already celebrated for his edifying discourses in the name of the Almighty. "[5]

But Jesus did not wish to marry at an early age and He left for India, the land of religions and famous yogis.

The tone and tenor of some passages in the parchment which are not included in the Bible are easily recognizable as the words of Jesus.

As an example, on one occasion, when Jesus was preaching in Palestine, an aged woman was pushed aside by one of the disguised spies of the Governor who placed himself before her.

Issa then said:

"It is not meet that a son should push aside his mother to occupy the first place which should be hers. Whosoever respecteth not his mother, the most sacred being next to God, is unworthy of the name of son.

Listen, therefore, to what I am about to say: Respect women, for she is the mother of the universe, and all the truth of divine creation dwells within her.

She is the basis of all that is good and beautiful, as she is also the germ of life and death. On her depends the entire existence of man, for she is his moral and natural support in all his works.

She gives you birth amid sufferings; by the sweat of her brow she watches over your growth, and until her death you cause her the most intense anguish. Bless her and adore her, for she is your only friend and support upon earth.

---

[5] ibid., Chapter IV: 10-11, p. 34

Respect her, protect her; in doing this, you will win her love and her heart, and you will be pleasing to God; for this shall many of your sins be remitted.

Do not expose her to humiliation; you would thereby humiliate yourself and lose the sentiment of love, without which nothing exists here below.

Protect your wife, that she may protect you and all your family; all you shall do for your mother, your wife, for a widow, or another woman in distress, you shall have done for God."[6]

Further examples:

"Do not worship idols, for they do not hear you; do not listen to the Vedas, where the truth is perverted; do not believe yourself first in all things, and do not humiliate your neighbor".[7]

"Not only must you desist from offering human sacrifice, but you must immolate no animal to which life has been given, for all things have been created for the benefit of men".[8]

"Do not take what belongs to others, for it would be robbing your neighbor of the goods he has acquired by the sweat of brow".[9]

"Deceive no one, that you may not yourself be deceived; strive to justify yourself the last judgment, for it will then be too late."[10]

Notovitch came back to Russia and prepared his manuscript and showed it to some well known ecclesiastics, but he was discouraged.

---

[6] ibid., Chapter XII: 9-21, p. 41
[7] ibid., Chapter V: 26, p. 35
[8] ibid., Chapter VII:14, p. 37
[9] ibid., Chapter VII:15, p. 37
[10] ibid., Chapter VII:16, p. 37

In Rome he met a powerful Cardinal and told him about his new manuscript, who advised him thus:

"Why should you print this? Nobody will attach much importance to it, and you will create numberless enemies thereby. You are still young however. If you need money, I can obtain some compensation for these notes, enough to remunerate you for your loss of time and expenditure".[11]

In Paris he met Cardinal Rottelli and his advice was:

"The Church suffers too deeply from this new current of atheistic ideas, and you would only furnish new food to the calumniators and detractors of the evangelical doctrine. I tell you this in the interest of all Christian Churches".[12]

Notovitch published his work, *The Unknown Life of Jesus Christ*, first in French in 1890 and in English in 1895 in London. The powerful Roman Church was totally against his work because it was against the teaching of the Church about Jesus' adulthood.

Many of the critics in the West were of different opinion. Some influential critics noted that Christianity had in some fields similarity with Buddhism, but they were not ready to accept Notovitch's version. Others even decided to discredit him arguing that Christianity had more credibility than Buddhism and the existing Church doctrines were the right ones. There was even accusation that the sojourn of Jesus in Tibet was a 'forgery and fraud'. There also came aggressive comments accusing him of forgery and even suggesting that Notovitch had never visited Hemis monastery and, therefore, what he wrote were all *worthless*.

---

[11] ibid., p. 10
[12] ibid., p. 10

Notovitch retorted with arguments and was even ready to go back to Hemis Monastery. He also mentioned:

"The Vatican Library possessed 63 complete or incomplete manuscripts, from India, China, Egypt and Arabia, in various languages, referring to Jesus".[13]

There were many attacks against the book but the most powerful shot came from Max Mueller, the famous authority on Indian Vedic Script and professor in Oxford University, in October 1894. Max Mueller was a distinguished and well respected personality in the Western world. He countered Notovitch with arguments and evidences from eyewitness report and came to the conclusion that Notovitch's findings were *worthless.*

It was a very hard blow for Notovitch, who observed that Professor Mueller's critique *"was an attempt to demolish me".*

Thereafter there was a long silence about Notovitch's findings concerning Jesus.

(Note: Notovitch had described his stay in a Monrovian Mission in Leh on his way to Hemis. A German doctor named Marx was heading the Mission and Notovitch stayed one night in the Mission. As normal in the Mission, Dr. Marx had written in the diary about the visit of Notovitch. In 1963 Professor Fida Hassnain got an opportunity to see the diary in the Mission and he took a photograph of it.)

Professor Fida Hassnain wrote:

"The revelations made by Notovitch became a red tag to the Christian Church and they made plans to refute his discovery and at the same time

---

[13] Hassnain, Prof. Fida: *A Search for the Historical Jesus*, Gateway Books, United Kingdom, 1994, Chapter 3, p. 30

steal these scrolls. .... Such attempts were made by the Christian Church in India also.

It has been the continuing practice of the Church to ... trace, buy, confiscate, and steal ancient documents referring inter alia *to Jesus' life in India, and his death in Cashmere"*.[14]

In 1890, after the publication of Notovitch's book in Europe, a Muslim named Ahamad Shah arrived in Hemis monastery. He also wanted to see the scrolls about Jesus and was denied. He was even ready to buy the scrolls and offered a huge sum of money. He stayed in Ladakh for almost four years and later wrote a book, **Four Years in Tibet**, describing his adventure and claiming that he was *authorized and paid* by the Christian Mission in India *"to refute the findings of Nicolas Notovitch"*.

3. Swami Abhedananda

Swami Abhedananda was a young friend of Swami Vivekananda and a disciple of Ramakrishna Paramahansa who spent many years in America as a preacher in Hindu philosophy. He also came in contact with Prof. Max Mueller and Prof. Paul Deussen, the famous German Sanskrit scholar.

Swami Abhedananda heard about Notovitch's findings and the arguments against it. He was skeptical about the version of Notovitch. But he did not participate in any discussion on the issue.

In 1921, he left America and returned to India. His main aim was to find out the truth about Notovitch's book about Jesus. In 1922 he visited Kashmir and from there went to Ladakh and the Hemis Monastery with a friend.

---

[14] ibid., Chapter 3, p. 33

That spiritual man was cordially welcomed by the chief lama to Hemis Monastery and he stayed for some days there. The chief lama was very happy to receive an Indian swami, a man of God. Swami Abhedananda politely asked the lama about the scrolls concerning Jesus and about the visit of Notovitch to the monastery. The lama confirmed both questions positively.

Something happened again. One day the chief lama explained the history of the scrolls and brought it from the library and Swami Abhedananda could read it with the help of a translator. He translated many verses from the scrolls into Bengali language. They were similar to the verses Notovitch translated and published in his book in 1890.

We could understand that the monastery was skeptical about the foreign visitors coming to see the documents. The chief lama kept it away from ordinary visitors to avoid any controversial discussions.

Later, Swami Prajnananda, a disciple of Swami Abhedananda, stated:

"I heard from his own lips that he (Abhedananda) saw the scrolls at Hemis and he translated from it."

Swami Abhedananda was a religious man and the chief lama was happy to show the scroll to the Indian Yogi. Swami Abhedananda, with the help of his assistant, published a book in Bengali in 1929 about his visit to Hemis titled, *Journey into Kashmir and Tibet.*

4. Nicholas Roerich

Nicolas Roerich was not only a famous Russian artist and painter, but also a keen archaeologist and explorer. He made elaborate expeditions to Kashmir, Ladakh, Tibet, the Himalayas and Mongolia.

During his expedition to Kashmir in 1925, he heard several stories about the life of Jesus in Kashmir. Ordinary people in Kashmir, Tibet and Ladakh were well informed about Jesus. They claimed that Jesus had come to Tibet and studied in the Buddhist Monasteries and preached to the common folk about God.

Roerich has recorded the accounts of a Hindu postmaster and several Buddhists in Leh claiming that Jesus had visited the area. According to their narration, there was a pond close to the bazaar where Jesus preached to the people standing under a tree. Roerich says legends about Jesus were extant among the ordinary people at so many places.

Those local people did not know about the book written by Notovitch but with *"deep reverence they speak of Issa"*. Issa was famous and His words were familiar to them as they heard it from their parents and grandparents.

> *"Many remember the lines from the book of Notovitch, but it is still more wonderful to discover, on this site, in several variants, the same version of the legend of Issa. One might wonder what relation Moslems, Hindus and Buddhists have with Issa."*[15]

Roerich recorded many words of Jesus he heard from local people; some of them are given below:

> *Jesus secretly left his parents and, together with a merchant, arrived in India 'to become perfected in the highest teaching. He passed His time in several ancient cities of India such as Benares. All loved him because Issa dwelt in peace with Vaishas and Shudras whom he instructed and helped.*

---

[15] Roerich, Nicolas: *Altai - Himalaya, A Travel Diary*, Adventures Unlimited Press, USA, Part IV, p. 89

Issa taught them:

- Worship not idols. Do not consider yourself first.

- Do not humiliate your neighbor. Help the poor.

- Sustain the feeble. Do evil to no one.

- Do not covet that which you do not possess and which is possessed by others

- Man should not strive to behold the Eternal Spirit with one's own eyes but to feel it with the heart, and to become a pure and worthy soul.

- Not only shall you not make human offerings, but you must not slaughter animals. Because all is given for the use of man.

- Do not cheat; you may in turn not be cheated.[16]

[It may be noted that sections of Hindu society, especially from rural pockets, until the middle of the 20th century, practised animal sacrifice and even human sacrifice (in which case, the prey was always from outside the caste system, an untouchable) to propitiate gods for special fanatic gains.]

Finally, Roerich came to the conclusion:

> *"But all versions agree on one point: That, during the time of His absence, Christ was in India and in Asia".*[17]

Nicolas Roerich was a religious person (but not a yogi) and he could speak the Tibetan language. So he got direct access to chief lamas in various Buddhist monasteries.

He visited the Hemis Monastery in the year 1922. In his book, *Altai Himalaya, a Travel Diary*, he described his meeting with the chief lama of Hemis and commented:

---

[16] ibid., Part IV, p. 91

[17] Roerich, Nicolas : *The Heart of Asia*, Inner Traditions International Ltd., Vermont, 1990, p. 24

"Regarding the legends of Jesus - first there was a complete denial. To our amazement denial first comes from the circle of missionaries. Then slowly, little by little, creep in fragmentary, reticent details, difficult to obtain. Finally it appears that, the old people in Ladakh have heard and know about the legends."[18]

Roerich gives detailed accounts of what he had heard about Jesus from the common people at different places. Many of the accounts were similar to the text translated by Notovitch in Hemis Monastery. It confirmed again that Notovitch had seen the original manuscripts existing in Hemis.

Roerich did not encounter much criticism from the academic circles when he published the book, probably because he was a famous person with a reputation for integrity and because he wrote what he really experienced. It was not easy to contradict or ridicule him.

5. Elizabeth G. Caspari

Madam Caspari was a Swiss professor in music. In 1939 Madam Caspari and her husband Charles made a religious expedition to Mount Kailas under the leadership of the internationally famous religious leader Mrs. Clarence Gasque. On the way to Kailas they wished to visit Hemis in order to participate in the three-day *Padma sambhava festival*. Unfortunately, they arrived at Hemis after the festival.

The lamas nevertheless received them cordially and even performed the rituals specially for them. One day, while relaxing on the roof of the monastery, they were approached by the librarian and two other monks. They brought three documents and one of them was opened in front of them and the librarian presented to the guests the parchment leaves saying, *"These books say your Jesus was here."[19]*

---

[18] Roerich, Nicholas: *Altai - Himalaya, A Travel Diary*, op.cit, part V, p. 114
[19] Prophet, Elizabeth Clare: *The Lost Years of Jesus*, Summit University Press, USA, 1984, p. 348

Though they were religious Christians, they had neither heard about the life of Jesus in India nor read the book written by Nicolas Notovitch nor had they known about the controversies that ensued the publication of Notovitch's book. They did not understand the Tibetan language, either.

They were surprised. But Madam Caspari took a photograph of the manuscript with the monk holding the scroll in his hand.

This is the only photograph known to exist of the manuscript about Jesus in Hemis Monastery.

That was also an evidence that the manuscript still existed in the Monastery until 1939.

6. The Aquarian Gospel of Jesus the Christ

The Aquarian Gospel was written by Levi H. Dowling. Levi was born in Ohio on May 18, 1844. At the age of eighteen he became a pastor and preacher and studied in the Northwestern Christian University at Indianapolis. He was a graduate of two medical colleges and practised medicine for a number of years. In his early life, he had a vision to '*build a white city*'. Later he became a yogi and meditated upon the theme for almost forty years. After deep meditation in the morning hours between two and six, he wrote *the Aquarian Gospel.*

He writes about the life of Jesus from birth till the crucifixion, including the hidden part of Jesus' life - His journey from Palestine to India, life in the Jagannath Temple in Puri, visit to Benares, preaching in different lands, the difficulties He confronted, His return - and eventual crucifixion in Palestine.

His story begins thus:

At the age of 13 Jesus was well known in Palestine and rich Jews wanted Him as their son in law. One day Jesus met an Indian prince named

Ravanna of Orissa and joined his caravan going to India and reached Sind. Later He arrived in Jagannath Temple in Puri where He was welcomed by the priests. He stayed there for four years and learned yoga, the Vedas and other Hindu scripts.

He learned the "Hindu art of healing and became the pupil of Udraka, greatest of the Hindu healers. "

Together with his teacher Udraka He visited Benares and other religious places in India.

In Katak in Orissa (Cuttack) at the riverside he taught the people.

One day there was a procession carrying the statue of *Jagannath* (deity of Krishna) accompanied by many cars (*radhams*) and followed by drunken people. As an onlooker, Jesus commented:

> *"Behold, a form without a spirit passes by; a body with no soul; a temple with no altar fires.*
> *This car of Krishna is an empty thing, for Krishna is not there.*
> *This car is an idol of a people drunk on wine of carnal things."*

He was totally against the *caste system* prevailing among the Hindus. He criticized the high caste Brahmins and taught the Sudras. Jesus said:

> *"Who in the boundlessness of love has made all men equal. The white, the black, the yellow and the red can look upon the face and say, Our father God."*

> *"The Sudra is the servant of the race of men; he has no rights that others need respect. And it means death to him to look into the face of priest, or king, and naught but death can free him from his state of servitude."*

In Benares, Jesus left the temple and stayed with the Sudras. He criticized the caste system prevailing in the society, which was formulated and propagated by the Brahmins.

The Brahmins became angry as He openly criticized the caste system and they planned to kill Him.

Jesus was warned and He secretly left for Buddhist centre *Kapilavastu* in Nepal, the birth place of the Buddha. There He learnt the Buddhist doctrines and rituals from the lamas.

Jesus travelled to Tibet and reached Lhasa and studied the Buddhist documents and holy scriptures in the Monastery. Then He travelled to Leh, the capital of Ladakh, and travelled in the villages and preached his *new faith.*

Here are some of the wonderful words of Jesus:

About the killing of all creatures with life, small or big:

> *"Now, men and birds and beasts and creeping things are deities, made of flesh; and how dare men kill anything?"*

About the Kingdom of God:

"The kingdom is not far away, but man with mortal eyes can see it not; it is within the heart."

To temple priests:

> *"When men array themselves in showy garbs to indicate that they are servants of the gods, and strut about like gaudy birds to be admired by men, because of piety or any other thing, the Holy One must surely turn away in sheer disgust."*

One day Jesus was preaching in Leh, in Ladakh, near the market,

> *"Not far away a woman lived, whose infant son was sick nigh unto death. The doctors had declared there is no hope; the child must die. The woman heard that Jesus was a teacher sent from God, and she believed that He had power to heal her son.*
>
> *And so she clasped the dying infant in her arms and ran with haste and asked to see the man of God.*
> *When Jesus saw her faith, He lifted up His eyes to heaven and said, 'My father –God, let power divine overshadow me, and let the Holy Breath fill full this child that it may live.'*
> *And in the presence of the multitude He laid his hand upon the child and said,*
> *'Good woman you are blest; your faith has saved your son'.*
> *And then the child was well."*

Many years had passed since He left Palestine. He learned the Vedas and many yoga techniques from the Hindus. He learned the Buddhist doctrines and travelled many parts in India, Tibet and Ladakh and finally decided to return to Palestine. On the way He visited Persia and was welcomed by the people.

In a small group of spiritual followers Jesus explains *the Silence* and how to enter it:

"There is a Silence where the soul may meet its God, and there the fount of wisdom is, and all who enter are immersed in light, and filled with wisdom, love and power. The Silence is not circumscribed; is not a place closed in with a wall, or rocky steeps, nor guarded by the sword of man!

"Men carry with them all the time the secret place where they may meet their God. It matters not where men abide, on mountain top, in deepest vale, in marts of trade, or in the quiet home; they may at once, at any

time, fling wide the door and find the Silence, find the house of God; it is within the soul".

(Look, how beautiful the lines are! We can see similar sentence in the Bible:

"The kingdom of God is within you.")

Jesus again teaches them *real yoga* explaining how a person can attain God during his life on earth.

"The Silence is the kingdom of the soul which is not seen by human eyes. When in the Silence, phantom forms may flirt before the mind; but they are all subservient to the will; the master soul may speak and they are gone.

If you would find this Silence of the soul, you must yourself prepare the way. None but the pure in heart may enter there. And you must lay aside all tenseness of mind, all business cares, all fears, all doubts and troubled thoughts.

Your human will must be absorbed by the divine; then you will come into a consciousness of holiness. You are within the Holy Place, and you will see upon a living shrine the candle of the Lord aflame.

And when you see it burning there, look deep within the temple of your brain, and you will see it all aglow. In every part, from head to foot, are candles all in place, just waiting to be lighted by the flaming torch of love. And when you see the candles all aflame, just look, and you will see, with eyes of soul, the waters of the fount of wisdom rushing on; and you may drink, and there abide." [20]

---

[20] H. Dowling, Levi: *The Aquarian Gospel of Jesus The Christ*, DeVorss & Co., Publishers, USA,1988, Chapter 40: 3, 5-7, 10-18 p. 63

So many years ago Jesus Christ taught His followers how to reach God by practicing *yoga* during one's life on earth. But Jesus follower, the Christian Church, left His teachings and taught us since centuries that one can attain God only after death; and the faithful folk still believe it blindly.

On His way back Jesus visited Assyria, Babylon and Greece and finally reached Egypt. He stayed for two years in the desert Monastery of the *Brotherhood* (belongs to Essene sect) in Egypt and finally returned to Palestine. Jesus was about 31 years of age.

Levi wrote also about the crucifixion of Jesus.

Levi wrote *the Aquarian Gospel* from his early morning visions. The most important significance of Levi's gospel is that he wrote about *the unknown life of Jesus in India, Nepal, Tibet and Ladakh* which was a fact unknown in Europe and never mentioned in the Bible. Significantly, it also records many of the words and parables He preached in foreign lands which the people there still remember.

It is not *glorious* to the Hindu Brahmins to hear that Jesus had vehemently criticized and opposed the (still existing) *caste system in India* and had supported the *Sudras*, the poorest in the society!

7. Other Sources of Information:

a. Jawaharlal Nehru, the first Prime Minister of India and a famous world historian of Kashmiri origin, wrote to his daughter, Indira, in a letter in 1932:
    "All over Central Asia, in Cashmere and Ladakh and Tibet and even farther north, there is still a strong belief that Jesus or Isa travelled about there."

b. Yogi Paramahansa Yogananda, founder of Self Realization Fellowship and disciple of Swami Sri Yukteshwar of Puri, told his disciples that Jesus visited and stayed in Jagannath Temple in Puri, Orissa.

There are four Shankaracharayas and they are the spiritual heads of Hinduism in India, each one similar to the Pope of the Roman Catholic Church.

In 1959 Sri Daya Mata of Self Realization Fellowship USA asked the spiritual leader, His Holiness Sri Bharathi Krishna Tirtha, the Shankaracharya of Puri, about the unknown years of Jesus in Puri. His Holiness replied:

"That is true. I have studied ancient records in the Puri Jagannath Temple confirming these facts. He was known as "Isha," and during part of his time in India he stayed in the Jagannath Temple. When he returned from this part of the world, he expounded the teachings that are known today as Christianity."

c.   Kanchi Shankaracharya Jayendra Sarswati

With respect to the film documentary, *Jesus in India,* the Associate Producer Anil Kumar Urmil got an opportunity for a rare interview with Kanchi Shankaracharya Jayendra Sarswati. In that interview the Shankaracharya gave some very important conclusions confirming the findings of Nicolas Notovitch.

"Also during the interview, the Shankaracharya totally laid to rest an objection that has been raised by those who do not believe that Jesus visited Jaganaath, as the Jesus Scrolls state that he did. Their objection stems from the fact that most accounts of the Jagannath Temple date the construction of the temple to the year AD 1174, over a thousand years after Jesus walked this earth. But the Shankaracharya, during the interview, states that Jagannath

Temple was first constructed in the year BC 483. The Temple was rebuilt in the year AD 1174".

The entire interview is given below:

Shankaracharya: I am the 145th Shankaracharya. Actually this tradition is 5000 years old, from the era of Sat Yuga. During the rapid spread of Buddhism, this tradition was suppressed. This first Shankaracharya was born in BC 506. **The Jagannath Temple was established as an education center in BC 483.**

Anil KumarUrmil: In the Christian New Testament there is hardly any mention of Jesus` life from 12 to 30. When Ed Martin asked about the Missing Years in his church, he was silenced.

Shankaracharya: The truth was submerged to propagate lies. Many important religious figures have come here to study. *Jesus Christ also came here to study.*

Anil KumarUrmil: So it is true He came here to study?

Shankaracharya: Yes, Yes.

Anil KumarUrmil: So Jesus Christ *did* study here for a few years?

Shankaracharya: He studied the Achar Samhita-the code of Conduct. He must have met the Shankaracharya of that time.

Anil KumarUrmil: Are there any ancient texts that have a record of this?

Shankaracharya: Our ancient records were buried some places here to protect them from invaders. That is why they are hard to find today. And even though we know these things, the Christians are not willing to believe it. **Jesus studied our teachings** of Truthfulness, Mercy, Charity; Serving Others, Compassion and Ethics. *The fact that Hindus made a contribution to Jesus' learning* is not accepted by some people.

Anil KumarUrmil: It is a fact that our very ancient Hindu text, the Bhavishya Maha Purana, has an account of King Shalivahana meeting Jesus in Kashmir, India.

Shankaracharya: Yes that is true, but the Christians will not believe it. Christians know Jesus was missing for many years. Where was he? Where was he living? Where was he traveling? *He lived in Kashmir. Travelled all over India. The truth has been covered up.*

There is one general question to be asked to the Indian historians and especially to the Hindu religious scholars:

Why didn't they, the learned Brahmins of India, write anything officially about Jesus in their texts though they had *liked and taught Him* and He was a *student of true Hinduism?*

The reason was simple: If they had written, they should have said the *whole truth* and not *the half truth*, which would be against their own interest. The mass was illiterate and they might have thought that they could hide the *truth* forever. *So thought also the Christian Church*

Chapter 5

Buddhism and Christianity

The Buddha was born about 563 years ago before Jesus was born. During the time of the Buddha and thereafter Hinduism was in decline and the society needed reform. The inhuman caste system practised by the higher class Brahmins in the Hindu society made the life of millions of lower class people miserable and unbearable. Besides the caste system, ritual animal sacrifices in temples as well as animal slaughter were the normal practice. The Buddha exhorted against all inhuman practices in society which were the root cause of the degeneration of Hinduism. His new principles presented in simple language showed the common man a new path of enlightenment and a new way of fashioning a peaceful society. His teachings worked for the betterment of society upholding *Ahimsa* and principles like *"love your neighbor as you love you"*, *"mercy to the animals and other creatures"*, etc. And he also taught how one could achieve enlightenment during one`s life on earth without *rebirth.*

The Buddhist monks were trained in yoga and practical medicine and they could heal the sick with their prayers. They led a simple life. They taught mercy to all creatures and were totally against animal slaughter, animal sacrifice and flesh eating. The result was a peaceful period in India, giving the common man more time for his spiritual advancement in life and Buddhism flourished all over the land. Many kings adopted Buddhism as their official religion and sent *missionaries* to neighbouring countries to propagate the new religion. The most famous Indian ruler, who adopted and propagated Buddhism, was Ashoka (BC 269-232).

Palestine had a pacifist sect known as the *Essenes* during the years before Jesus Christ, which survived until the third quarter of the first century. The

Essenes led a simple life similar to the Buddhist way of life. The people wore white and were always ready to help others and were peace loving. They were agriculturists in general and ate only vegetarian food. They were against animal slaughter and preached mercy towards all creatures. The monks among them observed celibacy and lived in monasteries. The monks practised yoga and medicine and maintained libraries with ancient documents. The group always remained together, protecting themselves from other sects under the Romans.

The Essenes were known by different names in Palestine, including:

> *The Sons of Peace, the Sect of the Scrolls, the Holy Ones, the Messianists, The Poor, The Meek, and The Elected.*

Ancient historian Josephus mentions about the Essenes in his book *Our War With the Romans* and gives a detailed description about their suffering under the Romans. He wrote:

"They scorn the miseries of life and are above pain, by the generosity of their mind. And as for death, if it be for their glory, they esteem it better than living always. Indeed, our war with the Romans gave abundant evidence what great souls they had in their trials, wherein they were tortured and distorted, burned and torn to pieces, and sent through all kinds of torture and torment, that they might blaspheme their legislator, or to eat what was forbidden to them, yet could they not be made to do either of them, no, nor once to flatter their tormentors, or to shed a tear. Rather, they smiled to their pains, and laughed those to scorn who inflicted the torments upon them, and resigned up their souls with great willingness as expecting to receive them again."[1]

Further, *"They are the most honest people in the world and are as good as their word, very industrious and enterprising, and they show great skill*

---

[1] Josephus: *Wars of Jews*, as quoted by Clary Ewing, Upton: *Prophet of the Red Sea Scrolls*, Tree of Life Publication, California 1993, Chapter 1, p. 38

and concern for agriculture. They exercise justice and equality in their dealings with all people. They (monks) never marry, and they keep no servants".[2]

They always greeted their brethren with the words, *peace be with you* or *peace be with your house.* One important matter concerning the Essenes was that they lived in the expectation of the coming of *"a Teacher of Righteousness".* The *Dead Sea Scrolls,* discovered in 1949, were the documents written and secretly kept in jars in caves in order to protect them from the Romans by the Essenes, when the Romans destroyed their famous monastery named Khirber Qumran in AD 70. The way the manuscripts were kept and protected in jars showed that it was foreseen not for a short period, but for a long period for the posterity in order to know the truth about the Essenes.

Upton Clary Ewing writes: *"They espoused a doctrine of non-violence which was unique among the Hebrews during the time of Jesus."[3]*

Prof. Fida Hassnain reminds us:

"There are many parallels between the doctrines of the Essene, formulated long before Jesus was born, and the early Christian doctrines. In the Dead Sea Scrolls there existed many teachings which in the Gospels are attributed to Jesus, but there is evidence that they stem from an ancient tradition."[4]

The English version of **Crucifixion by an Eyewitness,** as published by John E. Richardson in 1907, states:

---

[2] Josephus: *The Antiquities of the Jews*; as quoted by Hassnain, Prof. Fida : *A Search for the Historical Jesus*, Gateway Books, UK 1994, Chapter 10, p. 96
[3] Ewing, Upton Clary : *Prophet of the Dead Sea Scrolls*, Tree of Life Publication, California 1993, Chapter 7, p. 101
[4] Hassnain, Prof. Fida : *A Search for the Historical Jesus*, Gateway Books, UK 1994, Chapter 10, p. 97

"Most of the members were agriculturists and gardeners, and assembled together to promote virtue and wisdom among themselves. Furthermore, they devoted themselves especially in higher degrees, to the art of healing, induced thereto through their studies of nature and art, and were well acquainted with the effects of most of the known plants and minerals for recruiting the human system. This knowledge they made useful by healing and comforting the sick.

According to their moral standing and ability, they were divided into four classes or degrees. In the first degree were especially adopted children (the Essene monks hardly ever married), but in case an adult wished to be admitted into their Order, it was necessary to go through a very severe moral trial for a term of three years.

It was strictly prohibited for a member of higher degree to divulge any of the secrets of his degree to any of lower rank.

At their meals they broke the bread and passed the cup, and worshipped Jehovah; but never made any sacrifice in the temple, but performed their ceremonies in their homes. They knew no higher values than to suffer and die for their belief."[5]

Edmond Szekely found a document in 1928, which was kept very secret in the Vatican and is known as the *Gospel of the Essenes* in Aramaic. Prof. Fida Hassnain writes about it:

In it Jesus is shown as a teacher of Righteousness who preaches renunciation, austerity, a simple life, high ideals and mental purification.

Here is a passage from this Gospel:

"One day, Jesus sat amidst people who listened to his words with amazement. He said:"Seek not the Law in your scriptures, for the Law is

---

[5] *Crucifixion by an Eyewitness*, published by John E. Richardson 1907, Preface

life, whereas the scriptures is dead. The Law is the living word of the living God to living prophets for living men. In everything that is life is the Law written. You find it in the grass, in the trees, in the river, in the mountain, in the birds of heaven, in the fishes of the sea, but seek it chiefly in yourselves. God did not write the Law in books, but in your heart and in your spirits.[6]

Jesus was aware of sensuality and its effects on normal man. It is very difficult to understand that at any time He asked His followers, especially His disciples, to observe celibacy.

In the *Book of Thomas* Jesus speaks against sensuality in these words:

"Woe to you with the fire of sensuality raging within you, for it is unquenchable. The fire will devour your flesh visibly and tear at your soul secretly."[7]

Jesus also preached mercy to animals and all other creatures because they are all created by God.

The Essenes never slaughtered animals either for sacrifice or for eating the flesh. One of the early Christian Fathers named Titus Flavius Clements (around 150-214), wrote:

Sacrifices were invented by men as a pretext for eating flesh.[8]

Moses' 6th Commandment prohibits killing: *"Thou shall not kill"* was valid for animals and human beings. But the Christian Church limited the 6th Commandment to human beings. But the Bible has a Prophet speaking thus:

---

[6] Forsstroem, Johan: *The King of the Jews*; as quoted by Hassnain, Prof. Fida, op. cit. Chapter 10, p.99

[7] ibid., Chapter 10, p. 100

[8] Williams, Howard: *Ethics of Diet*; as quoted by Ewing, Upton Clary, op. cit.Chapter 9, p.139

He who slaughters an ox is like him who kills a man (Isaiah 66:3).

The Essenes were pure vegetarians and they neither drank wine nor sacrificed animals.

In the *Gospel of the Hebrews* (written by James the Just, Jesus' brother), Jesus pronounced on the torture and torment of animals:

"Let all know that God giveth grains and fruits of the earth for food, both to men and beasts. Those whose hands are stained with blood and whose mouths are defiled with the flesh of innocent creatures are not worthy of life in this world nor in the world to come."[9]

When Jesus was teaching his disciples in the temple, one of them asked: *Can blood sacrifices wash away sins?*

Jesus answered:

"No bloody sacrifices of animals or humans can ever wash away sins, and for few could a fault become eradicated through the shedding of innocent blood. He who kills kills himself, and who so eats the flesh of slain beasts eats of the body of death."[10]

Josephus, the historian, wrote about the Essenes as, *"The most perfect of all the sects in Palestine"*.

Prof. Fida Hassnain writes further:

"Members of the order embraced non-violence and enjoyed a high moral reputation amongst the Jews. They were vegetarians, and did not believe in animal sacrifice. All these lead us to believe that the Essene could be

---

[9] Forsstroem, Johan: *The King of the Jews*; as quoted by Hassnain, Prof. Fida, op. cit. Chapter 10, p.100

[10] ibid., Chapter 10, p.100

the Buddhists of western stock, maintaining secrecy over their identity or influence."[11]

Quoting Hegesippus (about AD 160) the Church Father Eusebius stated that James, the Lord`s brother, drunk no wine, nor ate the flesh of animals.

An early Christian centaury Christian document, *"presents Thomas as fasting, wearing a single (probably white) garment, giving what he has to others, and abstaining from the eating of flesh and the drinking of wine."[12]*

There are Church Fathers who say that Jesus also ate meat and that they only followed it. It is illogical and unimaginable to understand how Jesus and his followers could eat flesh of innocent animals. Jesus was born as the Son of God, the creator of the universe. God has no partiality to one of His creatures. For Him all His creations are equal and He is the Father of all. How is it possible for Jesus to allow eating the flesh of animals that His Father gave life to? The texts given in various Chapters show Jesus' reaction to flesh eaters as well as to human sacrifices which existed in the society. Indeed, animal slaughter and flesh eating were introduced in the Roman Church many years later by powerful pagan kings who accepted Christianity. They wanted to follow what they had practised before they became Christians.

There was another group called *Brotherhood* similar to the Essene, who lived in monasteries in the desert in Egypt. They were the *chosen ones* and were also known as *Therapeutae* who were profound in higher degree of spirituality; they were real *yogis.*

There were many similarities between the Essenes and Brotherhood that one could come to the conclusion that they belonged together.

---

[11] Josephus ; as quoted by Hassnain, Prof. Fida : op.cit, p. 57
[12] Bartlett, James Veron M.A: *The Apocryphal Gospels*; as quoted by Ewing, Upton Clary : op. cit., Chapter 9, p. 147

It was very important to know that Joseph and Mary were Essenes. Even during their stay with Jesus in Egypt, the family lived under the protection and supervision of the Essenes and Brotherhood.

Professor Hassnain writes:

"Through profound studies of mysteries of life and creation, they became attuned to the 'Will and the works of God' in nature, and were privileged to partake of the many health-giving secrets hidden therein. In consequence, they gained particular knowledge of certain roots and herbs from which they obtained various extracts and oils to heal the sick. Comparable to those of the brotherhood of Egypt whom Philo called the 'Therapeutae' (physicians or healers) they performed through the 'will' and the abounding gifts of Providence many remarkable cures, even to the raising up of those who had taken on the appearance of death."[13]

Considering all the facts given above and analyzing them without prejudice offer one comes to the conclusion that the early *Essenes* in Palestine and *Therapeutae* and *Brotherhood* in Egypt were people who believed in and practised original Buddhism. They came to Palestine many years before Jesus was born. They were the real followers of the Buddha and later the original Christians of the early Church in Palestine.

It is also important to note the words of the chief lama to Nicolas Notovitch in 1887 in the Buddhist Monastery in Mulbeck:

"The only error of the Christians is that after adopting the great doctrine of Buddha, they, at the very outset, completely separated themselves from him and created another Dalai-Lama; while ours alone has received the divine favor of seeing the majesty of Buddha face to face, and the power of serving as intermediary between heaven and earth".[14]

---

[13] Ewing, Upton Clary : op.cit., p. 28
[14] Notovitch, Nicolas : *The Unknown Life of Jesus Christ*, Tree of Life

Here the reference to *another Dalai-Lama* is the Pope, the head of the Roman Church.

Similarities Between Buddhism and the Church:

- The monastic life of the priests and the hierarchy in the Church from the Pope down to the priests was similar.

- The missionary work in their own and foreign countries had existed in the Buddhist period in India, which one could see later in the Church.

- 'The Heaven is within you' was a principle that existed in Buddhist teachings. They showed the way to attain it. Jesus also preached the same. The Church was using the same words since centuries and is still using it even today, but it lost *the way to show* its followers how to attain it.

- *"Love your neighbor as you love you"* was a common preaching text that existed in Buddhism, Hinduism and Christianity. Shankaracharya, the reformer of Hinduism, also advocated and really explained the meaning of that principle.

- *Whosoever shall smite thee on thy right cheek, turn to him the other also,* existed in both religions.

- The notion of incarnation and belief in rebirth existed in both religions. (*Emperor Justinian called for the Fifth Ecumenical Council of Constantinople in AD 553 with the main purpose of condemning the dogmas of reincarnation and rebirth existed in the church*).

- The Buddha and Jesus experienced the same `test of temptation` by Satan in their lives.

Publications Joshua Tree, California 1996, p. 20

- Alms, prayers, and sacrifices (not animals) for the dead existed in both religions.

- Priests took the vow of poverty, obedience and chastity in both religions.

- Priests and Lamas were empowered to accept confessions, impose penances and give absolution.

- Both used holy water.

There are many similarities between Buddhism and the early Christian Church. It is very important to analyze and find out why there are so many similarities between these two religions though the founders of both religions lived far apart. We know from history that during the time of Emperor Ashoka, the golden age of Buddhism in India, Buddhist missionaries were sent to various parts of the world. But no other two religions have as many similarities as between Buddhism and early Christianity. Finally, one comes to the conclusion that the Essenes were really Buddhists who came to Palestine about 250 years ago before the birth of Christ. One is compelled to believe that the Buddha and Jesus Christ were sent by the same Father to redeem the people on earth. In Buddhism as well as in Christianity we see the Buddha and Jesus as two *teachers of Righteousness.*

Indian Philosopher Dr. S. Radhakrishnan says, *"Two centuries before the Christian era, Buddhism closed in on Palestine. The Essenes, the Mandeans, and the Nazarite sects are filled with its spirit."*[15]

Owing to the similarities between the two religions, Sir William Monier, a scholar of Buddhism, wrote:

---

[15] Radhakrishnan, Dr. S.: *Eastern Religions and Western Thought;* as quoted by Bharat, Sandy: *Christ Across the Ganges*, O Books, 2007, UK, Chapter 2, p. 39

"Buddhism is the Christianity of the East and as such is in better conservation than Christianity, the Buddhism of the West."[16]

Concluding in the words of Upton Clary Ewing:

"All efforts made by the Church both past and present to becloud the case at hand merely reveals a prejudice which, for reasons more sensual than spiritual, is fearful of the truth."[17]

---

[16] Williams, Sir Monier: *The Mistory of the Ages*; as quoted by Hassnain, Prof. Fida, op. cit. Chapter 20, p.219
[17] Ewing, Upton Clary: op. cit., p.108

Chapter 6

Crucifixion and Resurrection

Detailed information has been given in the New Testament about the way Jesus was crucified. It was stated that Jesus died on the cross and His body was taken down and the wounds were washed with special oil and covered in a shawl and put in a sepulcher meant for Joseph of Arimathea. And they put a heavy stone at the entrance. After three days, Jesus resurrected and appeared before His disciples and finally, after three months, He bodily ascended to heaven.

Those were the common dogmas propagated by the Roman Church since centuries. It is a fact and accepted by many theologians that the Bible we now have is not the original version. Many a time in the history of the Church until 700 years after the crucifixion the existing copies of the Bible were burnt and forbidden to read. Many texts were manipulated and rewritten to make it suitable for the newly converted and powerful emperors and Church hierarchy. Any attempts to bring back the truth were fought back by the Church aggressively in all European countries. Whatever tricks suitable to suppress the truth, without any moral obligation or mercy, were acceptable for the Church. As explained in Bhagavad Gita, *"Both the **aim** and the **way** selected to attain the **aim** should be correct"*. If one of them failed, the achievements attained would become worthless after a period of time. In the case of Jesus` death, resurrection and ascension, the selected *aim* and the selected *way* to achieve the aim were wrong. Jesus is not responsible for that tragedy; but the Roman Church is.

The Roman Church did not have the integrity to tell the truth about Jesus, under whose banner it flourished on all continents, as to what happened to Him after the crucifixion and where He lived and died.

The resurrection of Jesus is one of the corner stones of the Christian faith. But there was doubt about the resurrection in the Church itself which was suppressed and bottled up in the Church Ecumenical Council in Nicaea in AD 325 under the reign of Emperor Constantine. Thereafter, resurrection became a Dogma and one who doubted or spoke against it would be fought back with the powerful weapon of *ex-communication* or expulsion from the Church. And *"by A.D. 328 all the Gospels in Hebrew language were ordered to be destroyed."[1]*

The earlier Christians were not believers in the resurrection of Christ. But St. Paul forcefully added it and reminded the Christians of Corinth:

"Now if Christ be preached that He rose from the dead, how say some among you that there is no resurrection of the dead? But if there is no resurrection of the dead, then Christ is not risen: and if Christ be not risen, then is our preaching in vain, and your faith is also in vain". (1 Corinthians 15: 12-14)

St. Paul wrote, *"Knowing that a man is not justified by the works of the Law, but by the faith of Jesus Christ"*. (Galatians 2:16).

St. Paul and his words were doctrinal in the 1st century of the Church.

But there were Christians who challenged St Paul's doctrine and James was one of them.

James, the brother of Jesus and head of the Church of Jerusalem, was the first to challenge the views of Paul. He says in his Epistle: *'Even so faith, if it hath not works, is dead, being alone. Thou believest that there is one God: thou doest well; the devils also believe, and tremble. But wilt thou know, O vain man, that faith without works is dead'*. (James 2:19-20)

---

[1] Faruqui, Mumtaz Ahamad : *The Crumbling of the Cross*, Ahmadiyya Anjuman Isha`at Islam, Lahore 1997, Chapter 10, p. 48

James was chosen as the leader of the Christians in Jerusalem and was executed by Roman emperor Herod Agrippa. James wrote also one Evangelium. But it was no more acceptable and did not exist in the modern Church history.

According to Bhagavad Gita, *Truth is one and is individable*, and there could not be 40 or 50 or even 80 per cent truth; it should be 100 percent. It is our born right as true believers in Jesus Christ to know the whole story after His crucifixion and not half the story.

In 1947, in a cave in the village Waldi Qumran, on the western shores of the Dead Sea, some very important scrolls, which were kept secretly in jars, were recovered unexpectedly.

"A Bedouin boy called Muhammad the Wolf was pursuing a stray goat on the Western shore of the Dead Sea. He noticed a cave in a cliff and threw a stone into it. There was the sound of breakage; he then climbed into it to investigate and found several tall jars in which there were rolled manuscripts. Thus was found the first of the Dead Sea Scrolls".[2]

In 1949 some parts of the Old Testament were recovered in Qumran cave.

"Many changes have taken place in the world since the day the Scrolls were hidden away for safekeeping 2,000 years ago."[3]

There were forty-nine documents including *The Gospel of Thomas and The Gospel of Philip* written in Aramaic, Jesus' mother tongue.

"It is clear from these Gospels that a large number of early Christians did not believe Jesus' death on the cross. In their opinion he 'first rose and then died' a natural death. It is also stated in these Gospels that, after

---

[2] *The Order of the Essenes Among the Jewish People,* Part II, p. 38
[3] Ewing, Upton Clary: *Prophet of Dead Sea Scrolls*, Tree of Life Publication, California 1993, Chapter 2, p. 44

crucifixion, Jesus remained in hiding with his disciples. During this period, he imparted special spiritual knowledge to Peter and James. After a period of about a year and a half, during which he instructed his disciples, he appointed James (his brother) as his successor and migrated to another country."[4]

Many texts existing in the Bible would convince that *"the gospel writers borrowed extensively from the Essene Scriptures"*.

There are many versions about Jesus after the crucifixion. Some of them are given below:

1. The Hindu version

India was the land of yogis and yoga. No country in the world has attained such a paramount level in the spiritual field. Only India can give an answer to *'what am I?'* India is the land of spiritual saints since centuries.

Jesus was a real *yogi* who attained his Christhood from India. After so many hours of painful punishment and crucifixion, it was possible for Jesus to undergo a *samadhi* without breathing giving the impression that he died.

According to *Natha-nama-vali* of the Nath Yogis of India, Jesus' life was different. They say:

"Isa Natha came to India at the age of fourteen. After this he returned to his own country and began preaching. Soon after, his brutish and materialistic countrymen conspired against him and had him crucified. After crucifixion, or perhaps even before it, Isa Natha entered Samadhi or profound trance, by means of yoga.

"Seeing him thus, the Jews presumed he was dead, and buried him in a tomb. At that very moment, however, one of his gurus or teachers, the

---

[4] Faruqui, Mumtaz Ahamad: op.cit., Chapter 13, p. 67

great Chetan Natha, happened to be in profound meditation, in the lower reaches of the Himalayas, and he saw in a vision the torture which Isa Natha was undergoing. He, therefore, made his body lighter than air and passed over to the land of Israel.

"The day of his arrival was marked with thunder and lightning, for the gods were angry with the Jews, and the whole world trembled. When Chetan Natha arrived, he took the body of Isa Natha from the tomb, woke him (Jesus) from his Samadhi, and later led him off to the sacred land of Aryans. Isa Natha then established an ashram in the lower regions of the Himalayas and he established the cult of the lingam and the yoni there".[5]

2. Muslim Version

In the Qur'an there are verses about Jesus. For example, about His birth:

"O Mary! Allah has chosen you and made you pure, and has preferred you above all women of creation. O Mary! Be obedient to your Lord, prostrate yourself and bow with those who bow in worship. O Mary! Allah gives you glad tidings of a word from Him, whose name is Messiah, Jesus son of Mary, illustrious in the world and the hereafter, and one of those brought near unto Allah. He will speak to mankind in His cradle and in His manhood, and He is of the righteous. She said: My Lord! 'How can I have a child when no mortal has touched me?' He said: 'So it will be. Allah creates what He will'." (Quran 3:42-47)

Not only does the Qur'an praise Mary but also rejects the death of Jesus on the cross. And to the people who believe in the death of Jesus on the cross, the Qur'an answers:

---

[5] Hassnain, Prof. Fida : *A Search for the Historical Jesus*, Gateway Books, UK 1994, Chapter 13, pp. 127-128

We have killed the Messiah, Jesus, son of Mary, Messenger of Allah, and they killed Him not, nor did they cause His death upon the cross, but He was made to appear to them as such. And certainly those who differ therein are in doubt about it. They have no (definite) knowledge about it, but only follow a conjecture; and they did not kill Him for certain: Nay, Allah exalted Him in His presence. And Allah is ever mighty and wise. (Quran Al Nisa 4:157-158)

The Qur'an also speaks about the Bible:

"And there is certainly a party of them who lie about the Book, that you may consider it to be (a part) of the Book while it is not (a part) of the Book; and they say, It is from Allah, while it is not from Allah; and they forge a lie against Allah while they know". (Quran 3:77)

But there are modern Islamic theologians and researchers who contradicted the death of Jesus on the cross with reasonable arguments. Some important authors among them are:

1. Hadhrat Mirza Ghulam Ahamad of Qadian (Book: *Jesus in India*)

2. Khwaja Nazir Ahamad (Book: *Jesus in Heaven on Earth*)

3. Professor Fida Hassnain (Book: *A Search for the Historical Jesus*)

4. Mumtaz Anjuman Faruqui (Book: *The Crumbling of the Cross*)

According to Muslim theologians, God the Father would never allow His son to die on the cross as a *criminal*. Death on the cross was a heinous punishment given to criminals in the Roman Empire. How could the Son of God die on the cross as a criminal? The Almighty God Father would never allow it. Jesus was sent to earth to redeem the sinners. He is the purest of all. He is pious and is ready to go through all punishments and crucifixion. Born as a man with flesh and blood normally would not wish to die. But he has to die because it is a natural law. On the cross He called His father to redeem him.

"Father, all things are possible unto Thee: take away this cup from me. Nevertheless, not what I will, but what Thou will". (Mark 14:36)

Jesus preached, "God is so merciful". Whatever His children faithfully ask, He gives.

"Ask, and it shall be given you, Seek, and you will find. Knock, and it will be opened to you. For every one that asks receives, And he who seeks finds, And to him who knocks it will be opened". (Matthew 7:7-8)

There is a logical question: How could such a God the Father allow His Son to die on the cross like a *criminal*? God Father would never allow it.

3. The Essene Version

In 1870 in an ancient house in Alexandria an old parchment written in Latin was discovered. A French literate wanted to keep the copy and at the same time a fanatic orthodox Jesuit missionary wanted to destroy it. But both of them failed to get the original document.

In 1873 this document was translated and published in German by a German translator. But after a short time the book was withdrawn from publication and even heard that the original document was destroyed and no copy would be available. So powerful was the order of Jesuit missionaries in Alexandria.

But in 1907 a copy of the German translation was accidentally found by the daughter of a Mason family in Massachusetts.

It is believed that the original Latin copy was taken to Germany by the Free Masons and is still under their possession.

After the crucifixion of Jesus, the Essenes Brotherhood in Alexandria was confused and wanted to get more information. The leader of the Brotherhood in Alexandria had written to the head of the Essenes brotherhood in Jerusalem asking for detailed information about the crucifixion and martyrdom of Jesus.

"As regards the discovered antique document, it consisted of a letter which the so called `Therapeut`(the elder), the highest esteemed member of the Brotherhood, had written to his brethren in Alexandria, in the name of Brotherhood of Jerusalem. This letter was written by him only a few years after the death of Jesus, giving a full description of the life, doctrine and death of Jesus, who the letter proves to have belonged to and been a member of their Brotherhood."[6]

4. The Crucifixion by an Eyewitness

It was a letter from the leader of the Essenes in Jerusalem to the leader of the Essenes Brethren in Alexandria *seven years* after the crucifixion of Jesus.

The author writes in the introduction:

"I write this to you, my Brethren, in the truth and knowledge of our Brotherhood, that you may know and understand the truth concerning what has come to pass. I tell you only of the things I know, and I have seen it all with my own eyes, and have taken a deep interest and an active part in all these transactions."

In the letter, the leader (*a Therapeut*) describes almost all the secrets kept about Jesus' crucifixion and what happened thereafter.

But he also mentioned in the letter that *"only the higher members had any knowledge about the secret assistance and protection Jesus received from us"*.

---

[6] *The Crucifixion by An Eyewitness*, Preface by Translator, Indo American Book Company, 1911, p. 7

According to the letter, the families of Mary and Joseph belonged to the Essenes sect. They protected the family since the birth of Jesus in Judaea and in Egypt. Jesus was educated and always protected by them. During the last three years of his life in Palestine, Jesus was always in contact with them.

"Therefore we have acted quietly and secretly, and have suffered the law to run its course; at the same time we secretly aided and assisted our friend in ways which did not infringe the law and our rules."

There are two men, as mentioned in the Bible, who played very important roles in the last days of Jesus; they are Joseph from Arimathea and Nicodemus. But the Bible did not tell us much about them.

Joseph from Arimathea was a rich Jew and a member of the powerful Roman Council. *"He was a prudent man, and while he did not appear to belong to any party, he was secretly a member of our sacred Order."* His friend Nicodemus *"was a modest learned man"*, but was holding *"the highest degree"* in the Essene Order.

The members of the Essenes Order had planned and prepared all kinds of precautions about what to do after the crucifixion. They did not want Jesus to die on the cross. They did have well organized connections in many fields, even with the soldiers. Everything was done as the law asked for; but everywhere they kept it in such a way that no harm was done to the life of Jesus.

After six hours of torture altogether Jesus became unconscious on the cross. In order to prove that he really died, one soldier took a spear and made a wound between his ribs, but it did *not go deep*; '*water and blood*' came out.

(*It is well known in modern medicine that no blood, but water will come out from a dead body if a wound is made. If blood had come out it shows that Jesus really did not die on the cross*).

Nicodemus shouted: *"We must immediately have the body with its bones unbroken, because he may still be saved."*

Joseph of Arimathea went to Pilate and secured the permission to bury the body.

Jewish law does not allow burial on Sabbath day, so the authorities were approached to have Jesus, who gave up His life on the cross on Friday buried immediately. (Indeed, the selection of the day for the crucifixion may also have been planned.)

Even the Roman centurion was a member of the Essenes sect. (According to history, he later became a bishop.)

Jesus` body was brought down from the cross and handed over to Joseph of Arimathea and Nicodemus.

"Nicodemus spread balsam in both the nail-pierced hands". They used other spices and salves which *"had great healing powers, and were used by our Essene Brethren who knew the medical science for the restoration to consciousness of those in a state of death-like fainting"*. The body was then laid in a sepulchre, which belonged to Joseph of Arimathea, and smoked *"with aloe and other strengthening herbs"* and a heavy stone was put in front of the entrance and they left.

There was a secret way from the sepulchre to the nearest monastery of the Essenes.

The angel, who appeared in white robe near the grave of Jesus, as stated in the Bible, was an Essene.

After almost thirty hours in the sepulchre, the Essenes knew, his body would become stronger and would wake up from deep sleep. Jesus woke up as expected and He was brought to the convent and secretly treated. He was not yet healthy.

He met Mary Magdalene, but she did not recognize him.

It was stated in the document that Mary was his consort.

The Brotherhood requested him to stay in the convent incognito as the Romans would again put him to death, if they came to know about his escape.

But Jesus said, *"The voice of God is more powerful within me than the fear of death. I will see my disciples once more, and will go to Galilee."*

He visited the secret house where some of the disciples (except Thomas) were in council. He met them, but they could not believe Him.

"But Jesus spoke to them, comforted them, and proved to them that He was really flesh and bones."

He was tired and took some rest. By asking for food, He wanted to convince them that He was alive. *"There was some bread, honey and fish of which He ate and refreshed himself."*

This convinced the disciples that He was the same master in flesh and blood and was not dead as they thought. They knew that a ghost would never eat bread or fish.

One of them who doubted the resurrection of Jesus was disciple Thomas. He was *"a deep thinker, who had received his education from the Essene brethren. Because of this, he possessed profound knowledge of the secret powers and process of nature"*. But Thomas reasoned with other disciples, *"not believing that a man can rise from the grave"*.

On the eighth day of his concealment, Jesus met all disciples, including Thomas, and *"Thomas was convinced"*.

He went to Mount Carmel and spoke with his disciples and followers. In order to avoid conflict again with the priestly class, He went to Bethania, to his mother, with Joseph and Nicodemus. Later He went to the 'Olive Mount'.

"And his soul was greatly moved, and his heart was filled with sadness, for he knew that this would be his last week."

He reached with his selected disciples near the summit of the Olive Mount from where he could see the land of Palestine. But the elders of the Brotherhood *"had silently come together on the other side of the mountain ready to travel".*

Jesus was sad and knew that He would not meet his followers any more.

"He prayed for the friends He was about to leave, and lifting his arms, He blessed them. And the mist rose around the mountain, tinted by descending sun."

The disciples knew that they had to spread His words to mankind, *"as he, their beloved, would return no more."*

This is the short description of the letter which is convincing and reasonable.

The *resurrection and ascension* of Jesus as taught by the Bible and the Roman Church are beyond logic and, therefore, not acceptable for a true believer of Jesus. Faith without conviction and human logic is not true faith. A normal member in the Roman Church, according to Church law, is supposed to believe everything without questioning the doctrines or dogmas. Such a *blind belief* does not touch or satisfy the soul. It is also a bad and traditional practice of the Roman Church to destroy any evidence existing against their teachings. The result is that a true believer remains far away from the Roman Church hierarchy and stays nearer to Jesus.

The preface to *The Crucifixion by an Eyewitness* stated that Mary Magdalene was Jesus' consort and that they usually kissed each other. What is the consequence of that truth on Jesus' believers? One is happy and can understand the Son of God better than the Jesus presented in the Bible. If the Son of God was born as a human being with flesh and blood, he naturally enjoyed sexual feelings as a normal human being. He possessed the power of God and the character of a human being with a human body. He was supposed to marry and live as an exemplary family man for the future generation.

In the case of Jesus, the Roman Church distorted the truth of His life as an adult and His long life after the crucifixion and put him in a Church made prison stating that His resurrection and ascension to heaven are beyond the imagination of normal human beings.

Where did Jesus go from Mount Olive?

Chapter 7

Return to Kashmir

Jesus was saved from the cross and lived in hiding because the Romans had learned that He had escaped death. There were two possibilities for Jesus, namely, preach again as He did earlier in Palestine and get caught, or save his life and leave the country unnoticed and fulfil his mission to preach among the *lost tribes.*

"I am not sent but unto the lost sheep of the house of Israel."

"For the son of man is come to save that which was lost."

Since we possess no evidence in any documents, including the Bible, that Jesus again preached in Palestine, we would believe that he selected the latter.

After bidding farewell to his disciples and faithful followers at Mount Olive, Jesus went to Damascus. At Damascus, He had a faithful follower named Ananias Abgar, who was an attendant of the King of Edessa. According to various documents, Jesus spent almost eighteen months in Damascus unnoticed and undiscovered. Around AD 37, Jesus met Paul, who was then known as Saul, face to face in Damascus where the Romans had sent him in pursuit of Jesus. At the end, Paul became a disciple of Jesus and later spread the Christian faith visiting Greece, Syria, Malta, Sicily and Rome.

Before Jesus left Palestine, James, his brother, was selected as the leader of the Christian community. The Romans wanted to suppress the new religious sect using force and executed James. Peter was put in prison, but he managed to escape. The disciples moved to Antioch in Syria as it was a secure place. There were some towns in Syria connected with the famous Silk Route and one among them was Nisibis.

"The Parthian empire stretched from Antioch and Palmira in the west to Kabul in the east, the Caspian Sea in the north and the Arabian Sea in the south".[1]

Thomas was sent in advance by Jesus to Parthia and India, safe places from the Romans.

But the Romans were still searching for Jesus. He left Damascus and reached Nisibis, a meeting place of caravans of different nationalities. In the book, *Rauzat al-Safa*, written in 1417, the author Mir Khwaz, mentioned about the concealment of Jesus in Nisibis under the name of Yuzu Asaph. The writer also mentioned about a walking *rod* which Jesus carried with him. That *rod* was very important because there were also mentions about that *rod* in Kashmir. Nisibis was under Parthians and Jesus could stay there. Ezad was the ruler of Nisibis and he was converted to the *new faith* by Ananias Abgar.

(Thereby hangs a story too: Ezad became very sick. Ananias heard about the preaching and healings of Jesus and he told Ezad about it. Ananias was sent to Jerusalem to bring Jesus and heal Ezad. When Ananias arrived in Jerusalem, he was informed by the disciples that Jesus had been crucified and died on the cross. A Jewish community was also living in Nisibis peacefully. According to the story, Thomas gave Ananias the shroud of Jesus and told him that the shroud would heal Ezad. As predicted by Thomas, Ezad was healed and he became a follower of Jesus.)

Jesus moved to Babylon, Ur and then arrived in the port town of Kharax and finally reached Persia.

In Persia he was known as Yuz Asaf as he cured the lepers there. In Persian Yuz Asaf means the seeker or leader of the lepers.

---

[1] Hassnain, Prof. Fida : *A Search for the Historical Jesus*, Gateway Books, UK 1994, Chapter 14, p. 147

From Persia, Jesus reached Kashgar. In old documents it was also stated that Jesus was accompanied by two women to the East, his mother Mary and his consort Mary Magdalene. According to the Gospel of Philip:

"There were three who always walked with the Lord: Mary his mother and her sister and Magdalene, the one who was called his companion. His sister and his mother and his companion were each a Mary".[2]

Six miles away from Kashgar there was a tomb dedicated to Mary Magdalene. Apparently, she could not withstand the rigours of the long travel and hardships experienced on the way.

Finally Jesus reached Kabul in Afghanistan. *"In Ghazni (Western Afghanistan) and in Jalalabad (in the extreme south-east of Afghanistan) there are two platforms which bear the name of Yuz Asaf, for he sat and preached there".*[3]

From Afghanistan Jesus travelled to Taxila, the capital of the Parthian kingdom, and the king was Gondaphorus. *"Taxila, during that period, occupied an important place on the trade routes between India, Central Asia and the Middle East".*[4]

It was to be noted that Thomas was sent to Taxila before Jesus in the year AD 40 and was well received by the king Gondaphorus.

There is a famous tomb existing in the name of Mary in the Murree Hills, about 45 km from Taxila and 50 km from Rawalpindi. *"Mary died on the way and was buried on a hilly place, which began to be known by her name and is now called Murree Hills. Originally the place was called Mari (a name by which Mary is called by Afghans, Jews and Cashmiris)".*[5]

---

[2] Gospel of Philip, as quoted by Hassnain, Prof. Fida: ibid., Chapter 15, p. 165
[3] Ahamad, Khwaja Nazir: *Jesus in Heaven on Earth,* Ammadiyya Anjuman Isha´at Islam, Lahore Inc. USA,1998, Chapter 24, p.387
[4] Hassnain, Prof. Fida: op. cit.; Chapter 15, p.159
[5] Faruqui, Mumtaz Ahamad: *The Crumbling of the Cross*, Ahmadiyya Anjuman Isha`at Islam, Lahore 1997, Chapter 14, p. 75

The name *Mari* remained *"until 1875, after which the spellings were changed to Murree"*.

Jesus and Thomas buried Mary in Murree Hills according to Jewish customs.

Mumtaz Ahamad Faruqui, who made research about the tomb of Mary, says:

"Hazarat Maryam (Mary, mother of Jesus) belongs to the priestly class of Israelites, hence it was befitting that that she be buried on a top of a hill(now called Pindi Point in Murree Hills). This grave, from what could be surmised, lay east and west in the Jewish style. The local old-time residents call it as "Mai Mari da Asthan" (the resting place of mother Mari (Mary)). The local Muslim populace used to come and make their offerings and pray. Some banners of different colours were also stuck there and earthen lamps used to be lit at the grave, especially on Thursdays, in fair weather."[6]

There is also an old belief still existing and practised: *"Whenever there was a drought in the region and they came and made offerings at the tomb and prayed for rain, the prayer was granted and the rains came. Now the tomb was converted into a regular shrine and on festivals like Shankaranat, the Hindus will bring* halwah *(sweet pudding) to the shrine and distribute it, and pray and lit earthen lamps on the grave at night time."*[7]

Thomas lived some years in Taxila together with Jesus. He learned from Jesus about the Jewish colonies existing in Malabar, in Kerala, and reached Cranganore in AD 52; the chief port was Muziris (the present Kodungallur).

---

[6] ibid., Chapter 14, pp. 75-76
[7] ibid., Chapter 14, p. 76

From Taxila, Jesus went to Kashmir. There is a valley named after Jesus called *Yusu Margh* in Kashmir through which Jesus entered Kashmir. *"There are about two dozen places in Cashmere which have the prefix "Isa" or Yusu (which is the oriental form of the name of Jesus)."*[8]

Jesus lived and preached in Kashmir and the people considered Him a holy man. He always carried a *rod* with Him and *"The rod or stick of Jesus (`Asa`-i-Isa`) has been mentioned in authentic and ancient book* Raudat-us-Safa *(Vol. 1, p 35) and in* Jama-u`t-Tawarikh *(Vol.2, page 81). According to Kashmiri traditions the possession of this `Rod` changed hands and places several times before it finally came to be deposited at the Shrine of Hazarat Zain -ud- Din Wali in Aish Muqam".*[9]

In Kashmir, Jesus was known as Yuzu, which derived from the Aramaic Jesu. In Urdu language also it is Yuzu.

Mulla Nadri writes in his work *Tarikh-i- Kashmir*:

"I have found in the ancient Hindu works that Issa, the Spirit of Allah, assumed the name of Yuzu Asaph in Cashmere."[10]

When Jesus arrived in Kashmir, Shalivahana was the king. There was a custom in the palace that the day to day official work done by the king was noted and written on bark papyrus by a special writer. That collection was called *Bhavishya Maha Purana*. The *Purana* (saga) was written in the Sharda script of ancient Kashmir. *"The present manuscript written by Sutta is a copy of the previous writings, and continuation from them. Sutta did this work around 115 AD".*[11]

---

[8] ibid., Chapter 15, p. 87
[9] ibid, Chapter 15, p.90
[10] Mulla Nadri, Tarik-i-Kasmir, as quoted by Hassnain, Prof Fida: op.cit, page 175
[11] Hassnain, Prof. Fida: op. cit., Chapter 18, p.198

Sutta recorded that in AD 78 the King Shalivahana left for the south to make more conquests. At Wyien, a place near to Pampur in Kashmir, *famous for its three mineral springs*, the king met a saintly person, fair in complexion, who wore a *long white robe*. In the conversation with the king he answered, who he was and where he came from.

As Prof. Fida Hassnain mentioned in his book, the translation of *Bhavishya Maha Purana* from ancient Kashmiri into English was made by Kashmir University professors. Professor Hassnain was not sure whether the king was Shalivahana or *"another person acting as the king of the Scythians and the year could be a little earlier than 78 AD"*. *Bhavishya Maha Purana* in English was published from the manuscript supplied by the Maharaja of Kashmir.

The translation is given below:

During this period, Shalivahana, grandson of Vikramaditya, laid hold on the kingdom of his father. He defeated the invincible Sakas (Scythians), and fought off the hordes from Cheen (China), Balhika (Bactria), Kamrupa (Parthia), Tatari(Mangolia), Roma (Rome - more probably Greece) and Khura (Khorasan).

He took possession of their treasures, and those who deserved punishment were punished. He also demarcated the border between the Aryans and the Mleechas (Amlekites), fixing Sindu (river Indus) as the boundary between the two peoples.

During this period, the king of the Sakas came to Himtunga (Himalaya). In the mountain area, Wyien, the king saw a dignified person of white complexion wearing a long white robe. Astonished to see this foreigner, he asked, who are you? The dignified person replied in a pleasant manner:

Know me as Ishvara Puthran or `Son of God`, Kanya Garbam, `Born of a Virgin`. Being given to truth and penances, I preach the truth to the Amlekites.

After hearing this, the king was astonished. He asked: Which religion do you preach? The dignified person replied: O king, I hail from the land far away, where there is no truth, and evil knows no limits. I appeared in the land of the Amlekites. I suffered at their hands.

I appeared as Isa Masih or Jesus Messiah. I received the Messiah-hood or Christ-hood.

I said unto them, "Remove all mental and bodily impurities. Recite the revealed prayer. Pray truthfully in the right manner. Obey the law. Remember the name of our Lord God. Meditate upon Him whose abode is in the centre of the sun."

When I appeared in the Amlekite country, I taught love, truth and purity of heart. I asked human beings to serve the Lord. But I suffered at the hands of the wicked and the guilty.

In truth, O King, all power rests with the Lord, who is in the centre of the sun. And the elements, and the cosmos, and the sun, and the God, are forever. Perfect, pure and blissful, God is always in my heart. Thus my name has been established as Isa Masih.

After having heard the pious words from the lips of the distinguished person, I felt peaceful, made obeisance to him and returned.[12]

According to documents and legends existing in Kashmir, Jesus had married and lived as a good husband and lovable father to his children. He died when he was about 117 years old. The tomb of Yuzu Asaph (Jesus) called *Roza Bal* is at Khanyar, in Srinagar, and his family members in the line of birth are responsible for the safeguarding of the tomb since centuries.

---

[12] *Bhavishya Maha Purana v.17-32*, as quoted by Hassnain, Prof. Fida: op. cit., Chapter 18, p. 200

There are many other evidences in Kashmir and in North India about Jewish settlements before Jesus arrived there. Tombs of Moses and Jesus had existed in Kashmir for centuries. But no evidence could be seen about the tombs of Moses or Jesus having ever existed in Egypt or Palestine, though they were, respectively, born there. There was a vacuum, long silence and illogical explanations based only on *belief.* Nobody in modern Israel or in the Roman Church is interested to know more. Israel has no interest or sympathy for the *ten lost tribes* because their followers in Afghanistan and Kashmir had converted to Islam and are now Muslims. The Church of Rome also has no interest to find out the *truth* because 1900 years of Church history shall have to be rewritten.

Upton Clary Ewing writes:

"Shameful as the fact seems to be, it has only been during the twentieth century that men have been free to read, write and express an opinion which might be considered embarrassing to canon law and practice without involving the hazard of being burned at a stake for heresy".[13]

The stories about Isa are known to the people in Kashmir, Ladakh and Tibet for generations through oral traditions and explanations. Such tales that one heard in the family and local society have long life in a period when writing had not developed or the habit of recording had not existed. It was the case with respect to St. Thomas in the Christian community of Kerala, India.

All the countries in the East had great cultures and riches. Hindu temples and Buddhist monasteries were the centres of spiritual yoga and art. Temples housed deities made of gold and adorned with jewels. Besides, the temples and monasteries were also the centres of learning and their libraries were filled with valuable documents. They were either looted or

---

[13] Ewing, Upton Clary: *Prophet of the Dead Sea Scrolls*, Tree of Life Publication, California 1993, Chapter 2, p. 47

destroyed by successive Muslim invaders who abhored idol worship or spirited away during European colonial rule that succeeded the Muslims.

In the Words of Professor Fida Hassnain:

"The vastness and richness of its various cultures can be seen from the treasures from this region which are now housed in the great museums of the world. Westerners have stolen caravan-loads of priceless treasures from the temples, mosques, tombs, caves and historical sites of Central Asia. Among the chief culprits, mention may be made of Aurel Stein of England, Albert von LeCoq of Germany, Sven Hedin of Sweden, Paul Pelliot of France, Langdon Warner of the United States and Otani of Japan.

In 1907, for example, Stein ravaged thousands of manuscripts and documents from the Tun-huang caves. These manuscripts were written in several Semitic alphabets. It is certain that some manuscripts written in Aramaic pertained to Jesus. Stein intentionally concealed this information from the world for the sake of the Church. He declared that these manuscripts embodied the teachings of Mani, which are similar to those of Jesus. His statement, though half true, served as a warning to the Church, who then deployed special missions to search out for destruction documents relating to Jesus. In this way a great deal of invaluable information about Jesus has been destroyed."[14]

---

[14] Hassnain, Prof. Fida: op. cit., Chapter 14, pp. 151-152

Chapter 8

Saint Thomas

We know from the Bible that Thomas was one of the disciples of Jesus who was initially not convinced about the resurrection of Jesus. The disciples thought that Jesus really had died on the cross and was buried in a sepulchre. Some days after the crucifixion, Jesus appeared before a group of disciples (except Thomas, who was away) and convinced them that he was alive and had not died by eating bread, fish and honey with them and reminding them that a *ghost does not eat.* Thomas heard the story but it was not rational for him to put faith above reason. As we learn from the Bible, Jesus met him later and convinced him that he was still alive with *flesh and blood* and had not died. That was the truth. The writings of Mark and Luke are really contradictory; on one hand Jesus tries hard to convince his disciples – by eating bread, fish and honey – that he was their same teacher still alive and not dead. On the other hand, the same Bible puts us in a difficult situation by declaring that Jesus had resurrected and *ascended to heaven with body* which is beyond reason.

Another surprising fact is that though Jesus had twelve Apostles, only the writings of Matthew, Luke, Mark and John have been included in the Bible. A natural and spontaneous question that would come up first is: were the remaining Apostles writings ignored or distorted or destroyed by the Church?

Mary was young when she was married to Joseph, who was much older than her. Mary and Joseph belonged to the pious sect of *Essenes* and they lived studiously observing the sect's moral codes. It was customary among the Jews in Palestine to marry off girls and boys by the age of 13 and 15, respectively.

It is logical to assume that Joseph was a widower when he married Mary. He had married as a young man of 15 and was blessed with children before his first wife died. He married again the young Mary and, according to the Bible, Jesus was the only child in the family. But there is good reason to think that Joseph had children in his first marriage and Mary also gave birth to children after the birth of Jesus and all of them lived together under the guidance of Mary and Joseph.

The Bible gives several references to the brothers of Jesus:

"Isn't he carpenter, the son of Mary, and the brother of James, Joseph, Judas and Simon?" (Mark 6:3)

Is not this the carpenter's son? Is not his mother called Mary? And are not his brothers James and Joseph and Simon and Judas? And are not all his sisters with us? Where then did this man get all this?" (Matthew 13:55-56)

So his brothers said to him, "Leave here and go to Judaea that your disciples may see the works you are doing. For no man works in secret if he seeks to be known openly. If you do these things, show yourself to the world." For even his brothers did not believe in him. Jesus said to them, "My time has not yet come, but your time is always here." (John 7: 3-6)

According to other Gospels, *James the Just* was Jesus` elder brother who became the Bishop of Jerusalem and was later executed by the Romans.

Acta Thomae, written in the 2nd century, is the surviving work which gives us more information about Thomas and his work in India.

Thomae is the Syriac form of Thomas. There were references showing Thomas was the brother of Jesus. They had similarities in appearance and *"often mistaken for each other by strangers"*.

According to *Acta Thomae* (The Acts of Thomas) his name was Didymos, meaning *twin,* and was called as *twin brother of Jesus.* Further, he was in possession of *secret knowledge*:

"Twin brother of Christ, apostle of the Highest, who shares in the knowledge of the hidden word of Christ, recipient of his secret pronouncements".[1]

That could be a reason why Thomas was sent to the Parthian Empire prior to the arrival of Jesus and Mary.

Considering the evidences we have from documents, Thomas had experience in architecture and was an expert in making buildings with stones.

There also existed deep sympathy and understanding between Jesus and Thomas. When Jesus planned to leave for India in secrecy, he sent Thomas in advance and followed him with another group later.

There was no mention about *Acta Thomae* in the Bible. But *"Acta Thomae was accepted and read as the Gospel of Thomas along with other canonical and apocryphal literature, in all churches until the Decree of Pope Galasius in AD 495 when it was condemned as heretical".[2]*

According to *Acta Thomae*, after the crucifixion, the Apostles selected the countries they wished to go by draw of lot in order to preach the *new faith* and Thomas got India. Thomas was unhappy and declined to fulfill the mission in India.

But obeying Jesus, Thomas sailed to India with an Indian merchant named Habban and reached the harbor of Sandaruk. Thomas became famous and won many devotees. Some years later he participated in the wedding ceremony of a princess. Judas Thomas was an important guest and gave good counsel to the newly wedded couple and blessed them. According to *Acta Thomae*:

---

[1] *Acta Thomae*, Chapter 39; as quoted by Hassnain, Prof. Fida: *A Search for the Historical Jesus*, Gateway Books, UK 1994, Chapter 15, p.158

[2] Faruqui, Mumtaz Ahamad: *The Crumbling of the Cross*, Ahmadiyya Anjuman Isha`at Islam, Lahore 1997, Chapter 14, p.70

"And the king requested the groom's man to go out of the bridal chamber, and when all the people had gone out, and the door of the bridal chamber was closed, the bridegroom raised the curtain, that he might bring the bride to himself. And he saw our Lord in the likeness of Judas (Thomas), standing and talking with the bride. The bridegroom said: 'Lo, thou didst go out at first, then how are thou still here'? Our Lord said to him: 'I am not Judas, but I am the brother of Judas'. And our Lord sat down on the bed, and let the young people sit down on the chairs, and began to speak to them."[3]

So on many occasions it was stated that Jesus and Thomas had close physical resemblance and sometimes strangers were confused to recognize them.

From several existing documents it could be accepted that after the crucifixion Jesus, mother Mary, Mary Magdalene and Thomas (Thomas left earlier than Jesus) left Palestine for India. Except Mary Magdalene, the others reached Taxila, capital of Parthia, during the reign of Gondaphorus. Gondaphorus ruled between AD 21 and 50.

According to available evidence, Thomas arrived in Taxila in AD 40 and met Gondaphorus and built the royal palace in 46 and Jesus arrived with his group in Taxila in 49.

There was also evidence to believe that Simon Peter also arrived in Taxila. Prof. Fida Hassnain the archaeologist has noted:

"At Charsadah near Taxila, archeological excavations have revealed many Christian antiquities, such as the statues of Thomas and Simon Peter, together with slabs bearing images of crucifixion. These archeological

---

[3] Klijin, A.F.J.: *The Acts of Thomas*; as quoted by Hassnain, Prof. Fida: op.cit., Chapter 15, p.161

excavations have established that Taxila was a centre of Christianity during the first century of AD".[4]

Other figures of foreigners were found at Julian in Taxila, where *"an Assyrian type of monastery was built by Julian, who accompanied Thomas during his travel to India. Near that monastery King Gondaphorus had ordered the construction of his palace, from where an Aramaic inscription has been excavated, which reads: 'A highly regarded foreign carpenter, who is a pious devotee of the Son of God, built this palace of cedar and ivory for the great king'."[5]*

St. Thomas met Jesus in the year AD 49 in Taxila. Many people followed Thomas to *the new faith* and he had many devotees in that area, including the brother of king Gondaphorus. Taxila became a center of Christianity in the Parthian empire.

"Much has been written and is known about Thomas in India, yet few people realize that Thomas was hardly alone in India. He shared his years in India with both Jesus and Apostle John and many other disciples and followers of Jesus. Many Hebrews and Christians were residents of India and established temples, churches and entire cities and communities together with the Brahmins. At one time Christianity and Buddhism were the most successful and predominant religions in India due, in part, to their teaching that all men are created equal. This presented a challenge for the Brahmin priests who adhered to strict caste guidelines or jati (cast) for each person; he/ she would have to live, marry and die each within his caste."[6]

---

[4] Hassnain, Prof. Fida: ibid. Chapter 15, p.159
[5] Qureshi, Molvi Mohammad Hamied: *Rahnuma-i-Taxila* (Urdu); as quoted by Hassnain, Prof. Fida: ibid. Chapter 15, p.159
[6] Hassnain, Prof. Fida and Olsson, Susanne : *Roza Bal, The Tomb of Jesus*, USA, 2004, Chapter 3, p. 43

It is worth noticing the many similarities in principles between Buddhism and Christianity. These two religions once existed harmoniously in northern India, keeping some common principles and working against the inhuman caste system that existed in the Hindu society. That could be the reason for the decline of Hinduism in India until the arrival of Shankaracharya.

Roman Emperors Constantine and Justinian were well wishers of the Christian Church. Indeed, the growth of Christianity in the Roman Empire began only with their patronage; but they dictated conditions for accepting Christianity as the common religion in the Empire. In the Council of Nicaea in the year AD 325, organized under the influence of Constantine, there were two groups of bishops, namely, those from the West and those from the East. The Easterners were not happy at the end because many of their beliefs were declared as heretical. Many of the principles followed by the faithful until then were cast away from Christianity. The Bible was manipulated and rewritten and declared as the only Book of Christianity. Copies of all other Gospels, including *Acta Thomae,* were *burnt* and *prohibited.* All beliefs held dear until then in the Roman Church which were not accepted by the Council were declared as heretical. There was a split in Christianity and Rome became the center of the powerful Christian Church. Rome sought to punish the Eastern Church and crush it. The Syrian Church in Edessa (the Thomas Christians), the Greek Church and the Coptic Church in Egypt belonged to the opposite camp. An interesting thing concerning Emperor Constantine was that he did not believe in Jesus. He merely wanted to cement his position in the Roman Empire with the help of the *new faith.* He received baptism just one hour before his death.

Large Jewish communities existed in Mumbai, Goa, Diu and the Malabar coast with headquarters at Cranganore (today's Kodungallur, which is believed to be the ancient port of Muziris) and Cochin. Probably, the first groups of Jews came to Cranganore during the time of the mass migration when the *ten tribes (Bani Israel)* moved to Parthia and later to various parts of India. South India already had commercial connections with Palestine as early as the time of Solomon.

During His first visit to India, Jesus had visited the centers where *the ten tribes* had settled in India, including Malabar (Malabar is part of Kerala), Ceylon (Sholabeth) and Ladakh, besides Afghanistan. After His arrival in Taxila in AD 49, Jesus asked Thomas to go to the Jewish communities in Malabar to spread the *new faith.*

"Thomas left Taxila and reached Kalyan (near Mumbai) and travelled along the western coast to reach Cranganore and nearby Palayur. He preached the new faith first to the Jewish community living in Palayur. Among the first converts were the famous four Jewish families of Palayur, namely Shankarapuri, Pakalomattam, Kalli and Kaliyankal. The first converts were not Brahmins, as people still believe in Kerala, but Jews living in Palayur."[7]

According to *Thoma Parvam,* a book of verse in Malayalam about the work of Thomas in Kerala, the Apostle visited Malabar twice; first in AD 52 when he stayed for only eight days and then after some years.

The Thomas Christians of Kerala claim their origins to Apostle Thomas, who also preached the *new faith* in neighbouring Tamil country and is believed to have been martyred at Mylapore in Madras (today's Chennai) in AD 71.

Mumtas Ahamad Faruqui, who made extensive research about Jesus' life in India and particularly Thomas Christians in Malabar, writes:

"They kept no images in their churches, and their ministers were allowed to marry."[8]

---

[7] Benhur, Abraham: *Jewish Background of Indian Christians,* Jeevanist Books, Calicut, 2011
[8] Faruqui, Mumtaz Ahamad: op.cit., Chapter 14, p. 72

Early Christianity did not keep images or statues in the churches. Neither did the Buddhists in their temples. Buddha was against worship of statues or images in temples when he lived.

Thoma Parvam gives more information:

"The song tells that Prince Peter or Kepha of Muziris, who was one of the Apostle's first converts, visited St. Thomas in the Pandya Kingdom (in Andhra Pradesh) and requested him to return to Malabar. The Apostle came first to the Coromandal coast and then, acceding to the request, accompanied Prince Kepha to Kerala, where he baptized members of the Cranganore royal family. Three thousand non-Christians received the faith and were baptized in the course of eighteen months. Among these converts there were forty members of the Jewish community, including Rabbi Paul of the Cranganore Synagogue, where every Saturday the Apostle used to go and read and explain the Old Testament for the Jewish congregation. Though Rabbi Paul received baptism and became a Christian, a good number of the Cranganore Jewish community continued to stick to their ancestral religion and gave the Christians the name 'Nazaranis', meaning followers of the man from Nazareth, i.e., Jesus Christ".

Kidangallor Evangelization

"Besides Jews, Brahmins, Kshatriyas, Nairs, and Chettiars were among the earliest converts to Christianity. The first Brahmin convert was a young member of a Niranom Brahmin family that had settled down in Cranganore, engaged in some business. The young man's conversion was not liked by his father, who decided to cast him away from the family. The Apostle called the young convert and asked him to live with him. The young man, who had received the Apostle's name in baptism agreed to live with him and came to be known as Thomas Maliyakal, in recognition of

his Brahmin family name. Subsequently, he was raised to priesthood, and after some time was given the title of Ramban or Arch-priest".[9]

The Jews who lived in Palayur and were opposed to the new faith, cursed Palayur and left for other regions. Thereafter the area, which included Palayur, was known as *Shaapakadu (accursed forest)*. Its present name, Chavakadu (Chowghat), comes close in meaning - *forest of the dead*.

The Christian community in Taxila and Kashmir did not last long. Prof. Fida Hassnain writes:

"This Christian community founded by Thomas in the first century (in Taxila) has continued up to present times. Later, the Hsiung-Nu (Hun) invasions of North India, around 430 AD, drove non-Hindu minorities in all directions, the Buddhists towards Ladakh, Tibet and the east, and the Jews and Christians to the south, especially Malabar. The Shaivite Hindus of the north were prepared to adapt their faith to the needs of the time, but these minorities were not prepared to do so – thus the Christian communities in Taxila and Cashmere died out."[10]

It is well known that the Thomas Christian community in Kerala lived peacefully respecting all other religions. They allowed their priests (ministers) to marry and they led an exemplary family life within the community. That custom was prohibited by the Portuguese bishops after the colonization beginning in AD 1498.

`Christian` treachery and persecution in Kerala.

"More than one unsuccessful attempt was made in the early centuries by the Mediterranean Christians to establish their form of Christianity in India. At the coming of the Europeans in large numbers, however, this began to change, culminating in a full-scale persecution by the Portuguese colonialists,

---

[9] Ramban, Thomas: *Thomas Parvam, The Songs of Thomas*, 1601
[10] Hassnain, Prof. Fida: op.cit., Chapter 14, p.162

who first came to India in 1498. Christians from Europe were always received in total friendship by the Christians of Saint Thomas and often given places to live. In many instances the Saint Thomas Christians interceded with the local rulers in gaining residency and trade permissions for the Europeans. But sadly, on the part of the opportunistic Europeans there was no such sincere openness, and as soon as any political ascendancy was attained, pressure would be brought to bear on the Saint Thomas Christians to convert to the Christianity of the Westerners.

This came to an appalling climax in the last year of the sixteenth century when the Portuguese Roman Catholic Archbishop of Goa, Alexius Menezes, summoned all the Saint Thomas Christian clergy and a considerable number of laymen to the town of Diamper to supposedly bring peace and reconciliation between the two churches. In response one hundred fifty-three priests and about six hundred and sixty laymen attended. The Saint Thomas Christians were asked to bring all their liturgical and theological texts–especially their ancient texts containing the teachings of Saint Thomas–so they could be "examined." Believing that the Europeans wanted to sincerely discover the apostolic traditions of Saint Thomas, and therefore of Jesus, they did so. Their horror was boundless when they found themselves surrounded by Portuguese soldiers who forced them at gunpoint to surrender their precious manuscripts, which were then burned in their presence at the order of the Archbishop. Because of this "It is not possible to write a complete history of the Christians in South-West India, because the ancient documents of their churches were destroyed by fire at the Synod of Diamper in 1599," as Cardinal Tisserant admits.

`What history will not willingly forgive is the literary holocaust which was carried out on the authority of this decree, when all books that could be laid hands on were consigned to the flames. It was comparable in many ways with the vandalism of Muslim Caliph Omar, who by similar wanton destruction ordered the noble library of Alexandria to be consumed by

flames. The Syrian Christians of today believe that because of this cruel decree, no records are available with them to recover and establish beyond all dispute their past Church history. None will deny that there is some substance in this belief ` (S. G. Pothen, book: The Syrian Christians of Kerala).

Among the books burned were many copies of three books. Two of them, The Book of Charms and The Ring of Solomon, were books of Christian magic. The third was a book on esoteric healing and the making of amulets from gems and herbs (as the Essenes had also done) called The Medicine of the Persians. They now exist only as nearly-forgotten names.

Not only were the books brought to Diamper destroyed, Archbishop Menezes went from church to church searching for more books and burning entire libraries in many places–even in areas where the Portuguese had no political power whatsoever. The liturgical texts containing the rites of the Chaldean tradition were especially sought out and destroyed because they revealed how utterly the other churches had departed from the original ways of Christianity, and because they expressed the correct view of Jesus as a Son of God by attainment and not as the creator God incarnate. A list of forbidden books was made at Diamper, and any who read or listened to them being read were automatically condemned.

Over the course of the next days the Archbishop also engaged in harangues to "correct" the ways of the Saint Thomas Christians and bring them into conformity with those of "the one, holy, catholic, and apostolic See of Rome." The Portuguese even forced the Christians of Saint Thomas to change the way they made the Sign of the Cross (right to left) to the way the Western Christians had only recently themselves come to do it (left to right) ".[11]

---

[11] Burke, George (Swami Nirmalananda Giri): *The Apostole of India*

Khwaja Nazir Ahamad writes about the magnificent ancient three cathedrals in Fort St. George (Madras) associated with Thomas:

"In another [cathedral], a portion of the spear with which the body of Thomas was pierced is even now preserved. In this church, certain inscriptions in Pahlavi are still to be found. In the third cathedral, a bust of Thomas is exhibited. This figure represents him as raising his right hand in benediction. In his left hand he holds a carpenter's square, associating him with the occupation of his father, Joseph, the carpenter".[12]

For the Church of Rome the existence of Christians in India in earlier centuries was not unknown.

"Ephraem (AD 306 -373) wrote of Thomas' mission in India, and Anorbius (around AD 305) listed India as Christian influenced. Then, one of the participants in the Council of Nicaea was a person called 'Bishop John of all Persia and Greater India'. (In some documents the participant is identified as Bishop Johannan, who could have been from Kerala as the name is common in Kerala). In around 335, Roman Emperor Constantine sent Bishop Theophios to India to reform the churches there."[13]

During the reign of Ashoka (BC 304 -232) Buddhism spread all over India and also in foreign countries. Between the 1st and 3rd centuries, the Thomas Christians, Jews, Buddhists and Hindus lived harmoniously in the Parthian Empire. The Thomas Christians expanded in the Empire, including Kashmir and Afghanistan. During that period Hinduism was in decline. Thereafter came the great Shankaracharya (AD 788-820) the redeemer of Hinduism.

There are some unanswered questions in the history of India about that

---

[12] Ahamad, Khwaja Nazir: *Jesus in Heaven on Earth*, Ammadiyya Anjuman Isha´ at Islam, Lahore Inc. USA,1998, Chapter 23, p. 370
[13] Hassnain, Pro. Fida: op.cit., Chapter 15, pp. 167-168

period. Hinduism began to decline gradually after the death of Buddha and Buddhism got priority in the reign of Emperor Ashoka. Later, the Buddhists, Hindus, Christians and Jews lived harmoniously.

"Why did they have great affinity with Buddhism but not with Hinduism? It may have had something to do with the Brahmins' emphasis on the caste system, something that the Hebrews, who were often regarded as second class citizens and slaves, and persecuted for it, would be loath to follow".[14]

Did Shankaracharya oppose the caste system existing in Hinduism? Shankaracharya was pious and a holy preacher and the most logical thinker ever born. All his thinking and arguments were based on reason and not on belief and superstition. Therefore, one can assume that Shankaracharya vehemently opposed the caste system, which was one of the root causes of the decline of Hinduism. After his death, the chief Acharyas in the four *maths* were responsible for guiding the reformed Hinduism.

Then comes the question: Why is there no reference in the history of India and the history of Hinduism to the Jewish people living in various parts of India since 500 BC nor to the presence of Christianity in Taxila in the Parthian Empire, nor a proper reference about the life of Jesus and Thomas in the Parthian empire? Modern excavations were made in Taxila, Julian (famous monastery) and in the vicinity of the palace of Gondaphorus. Many foreign figures were found from all these places. It was also concluded that the palace of Gondaphorus was built by *a foreign architect.* They had ample evidence, but they were never mentioned in the modern Indian history.

One can only conclude that the learned Hindu religious priests as well as Hindu historians (obviously Brahmins, because only Brahmins were allowed to learn and write in those days) had purposely suppressed that

---

[14] Hassnain, Prof. Fida and Olsson, Susanne: op.cit., Chapter 6, p.131

valuable information from the Indian people because it would affect the prestige of the Hindu religion.

"And yet to this day Hindus give only the barest acknowledgement that Christians 'might' have been in India since the days of Jesus. The Jews were there in large numbers at least five hundred years before Jesus".[15]

Even the Roman Church, which was founded in the name of Jesus and knew the whole history, also lied and suppressed the truth. The Church did it because it brought new dogmas, namely *the Resurrection and Ascension* of Jesus, around the 3rd century. If the world had learned about the work of Jesus and Thomas in the Parthian Empire in the first century, it would have put a spoke in the teachings of the Roman Church. So the Church tried its best to obliterate the truth by buying and burning all documents it could get concerning Jesus and Thomas with respect to their life in Parthian Empire.

It is inexcusable.

There are some cruel parallels in Hinduism and Christianity. The *caste* system in Hinduism (it could neither be seen nor touched) since centuries made the life of millions of innocent *Hindus* miserable. They were born as human beings, suffered so many cruelties in life. Only death freed them from their miseries.

It was many years after the crucifixion of Christ that the emperors and kings of Europe and, automatically, the common people in their kingdoms became Christian. The Roman Church became very powerful in Europe. There existed a powerful relationship between the Pope in the Vatican and the kings in Europe. Each side tried their best to consolidate power by employing ways that suited them. They also sometimes fought against each other killing so many people. In the Middle Ages, they tortured and

---

[15] Hassnain, Prof. Fida and Olsson: ibit., Chapter 3, p. 59

executed thousands of innocent Christian men and women, including even theologians, employing the powerful weapons of *Inquisition* and *Witch-hunt*, which several Popes accepted and approved.

The famous Indian Philosopher, Dr. S. Radhakrishnan, was convinced to say:

"If He (Jesus) had returned to Europe in the Middle Ages, He would certainly have been burnt alive for denying the dogmas about His own nature".[16]

The Pope in Vatican apportioned the continents for European Christian kings to colonize and propagate the *new faith* to the countries in Asia, the Americas, Africa and Australia. In all those countries people lived peacefully and harmoniously for centuries upholding their old religions, culture and advanced civilizations. The *new faith* founded by Jesus and propagated by Thomas still existed in India. But the Christian fanatics from Europe had only one motive: loot the riches of these countries and keep innocent people under colonial yoke.

The practice of *slavery* in the European colonies in Africa and South America and in the United States of America made the life of millions of innocent people miserable and unbearable.

They sold innocent men and women from Africa to North American plantation owners as *slaves* without respecting human dignity. The Christian Church even descended to the level of asserting that the *"black man has no soul"* and is, therefore, not human. The African slaves in North America were treated so harshly, especially on Sundays, by their God-fearing Sunday Church-going *Christian Slave Masters* and gave them a status lower than cattle. It is very revealing to read the speech of *free slave Frederic Douglas* on 4th of July 1774 against the atrocities and inhuman life of the slaves in independent North America.

---

[16] Radhakrishnan, Dr. S. : *Eastern Religions and Western Thought*; as quoted by Bharat, Sandy: *Christ Across the Ganges*, O Books, 2007, UK, Chapter 2, p. 37

The irony of the fact is: all those atrocities were condoned by the Church founded on the teachings of Jesus Christ, the Son of God. In reality, the Church was repudiating Jesus and doing everything against His teachings.

In short, the *aim* and the *way* the Church selected to reach the people in other continents were both brutally wrong.

Chapter 9

Tomb of Jesus `Roza Bal` at Khanyar in Srinagar, Kashmir

After staying some years in Taxila, Jesus went to Kashmir, the place where he really wanted to settle down. Kashmir is a place specially blessed by God with marvelous mountains and green valleys, rivers and lakes, forests and snow, birds and animals. Many writers have complimented Kashmir describing it as *paradise on earth*. Many of the inhabitants living there in the 3rd century BC belonged to the family of the *lost sheep of Israel*, followers of the Jewish religion. Many of the places mentioned in the Old Testament, according to archaeologists, are in Kashmir.

The Kashmiris believe that Moses had come to Kashmir in his old age and died in Kashmir. (For details refer to: *Jesus Lived in India* by Holger Kersten, Penguin Books, New Delhi, India).

Jesus started his mission in Kashmir in the year AD 78, arriving from Taxila and passing through *Yusu Marg,* which was named after Him. Jesus and his companions found a shelter in an old Buddhist monastery on a hill in *Aish Muqam*. According to the history of Kashmir, Jesus wore *"cloths of white fleece and a turban (a common head wrap to keep road dust off clean hair; the style was first pictured in use by Egyptians) and carried a rod in his hand."* [1]

He preached his *new faith* to the people of Kashmir wandering in the valley and died in Kashmir around the age of 117.

Al-Sheikh Al- Said-us-Sadiq was a famous scholar and traveller to many countries who died in AD 926. He wrote in his famous book, *Kamal-uddin*

---

[1] Faqir Mohammad: *Jamia-at-Tawarikh* (AD1863); as quoted by Hassnain, Prof. Fida & Olsson, Suzanne: *Roza Bal, The Tomb of Jesus*, USA, 2004, Chapter 4, p.79

Tmam-un Nimat fi Asbat-ul Ghaibat wa Kashf-ul-Hairet, about Jesus'
teachings in Kashmir. Here are two of them:

*"O people! Heed my words: they are of truth and wisdom: they will enable
        you to distinguish between right and wrong. This indeed is the
        religion of the Prophets of yore....Whoever will discard it he shall
        not enter heaven. Seek not the kingdom of this world but rather
        that of heaven.... the earthly kingdom and happiness is to end and
        those who seek them shall perish.... The time (of death) is nigh.
        The birds have no control over their enemies. So have you none
        without faith and works.... So long as there is light, travel
        therein.... But keep your good deeds secret from people (lest they
        be for show only) .... Treat others as you would like to be treated,
        shun worldly desire, give up calumny, anger and back
        biting....your minds and actions should be pure and identical... ".*

*"When a sower goes to sow and sows, some seed fall by wayside, and
        the birds pick up the seeds. Some fall upon the stray land, and
        when they reach the stony foundation they wither away. Some
        fall among thorns and grow not: but the seed which falls on the
        good land grows and brings forth fruit. By the sower is meant
        the wise, by seed is meant his words of wisdom. The seeds picked
        up by the birds mean those people who understand not. The seed
        on the stony ground are like the words of wisdom which go in
        one ear and out of the other. The seed which fell among thorns
        are like unto those who hear and understand but act not
        accordingly. Other seeds which fall on good ground are like
        those who hear the words of wisdom and obey."[2]*

Every Christian is familiar with that parable of Jesus.

---

[2] Al-Sheikh Al- Said-us-Sadiq: *Ikmal-ud-Din*; as quoted by Mohamad, Khwaja
Nazir: *Jesus in Heaven on Earth*, Ammadiyya Anjuman Isha´ at Islam, Lahore
Inc. USA,1998, Chapter 24, p.399

Early Christians in Persia and North West India were called *Nassara* and some groups were called *Kristianis* (The name *Christianis* is also used the Thomas Christians in Kerala). The Christians in Kashmir are called *Kri*. Many of the people living in Afghanistan, especially in Herath, had belonged to the Jewish origin.

Jesus initially lived as a bachelor in Kashmir. One day, after a meeting with the king of Kashmir, He was chided by the king:

"For neglecting himself and not having a wife to look after his needs. The king urged him to meet Marjan of Pahalgam, his first choice from among several local women, and at the king's insistence they were married".[3]

Marjan could be of Jewish origin because *"Kashmir valley was guarded jealously by Jews and only Jews who were known to them were permitted residency".*[4]

He begot a son named *Eli-Kim* from Marjan.

Al-Sheikh Al-Said-us-Sadiq wrote:

"Then Yuzu Asaph, after roaming in many cities, reached that country which is called Kashmir. He travelled in it far and wide, and stayed there and spent his (roaming) life there, until death overtook him, and he left the earthly body and was elevated towards the Light. But before his death, he sent for a disciple of his, Ba'bad, (Thomas) by name, who used to serve him and was well versed in all matters. He (Yuzu Asaph) expressed his last wish to him and said, 'My time for departing from this world has come.

---

[3] Faber- Kaiser, Andreas: *Jesus Died in Kashmir*; as quoted by Hassnain, Prof. Fida & Olsson, Suzanne, op.cit., Chapter 4, p. 84
[4] Hassnain, Prof. Fida & Olsson, Suzanne: *Roza Bal, The Tomb of Jesus*, USA, 2004, Chapter 4, p. 77

Carry on your duties properly and turn not back from truth, and say your prayers regularly.' He then directed Ba 'bad to prepare a tomb over him at the very place he died. He then stretched his legs towards the west and head towards the east and died. May God bless him?"[5]

John was the beloved disciple of Jesus who lived and preached in Asia Minor. He is the patron saint of Asia Minor in the Roman Church. He had a long life and was the only Apostle who died a natural death.

According to history, Thomas was killed in Mylapur, in Chennai (former name Madras), in AD 71. Therefore, the disciple Jesus summoned to witness his death could be Apostle John, and not Thomas (*Ba 'bad*).

Mulla Nadir, who wrote the History of Kashmir (*Tarikh-i-Kashmir*) in Persian in AD 1420, recorded that Hazarat Yuzu Asaph (Jesus) came from Bait-ul-Muqadas (meaning Holy House of Jerusalem) and reached Kashmir during the reign of Raja Gopananda who ruled between AD 49 and 109.

Francis Younghusband, a representative of British Administration in Kashmir for many years, wrote:

> *"There resided in Kashmir some 1900 years ago a saint of the name of Yuz Asaf, who preached in parables and used many of the same parables as Christ used, as, for instance, the parable of the sower. His tomb is in Srinagar.... And the theory is that Yuz Asaf and Jesus are one and the same person. When the people are in appearance in such a decided Jewish cast, it is curious that such a theory should exist".*[6]

---

[5] Al-Sheikh Al- Said-us-Sadiq: *Ikmal-ud-Din*; as quoted by Mohamad, Khwaja Nazir, op. cit., Chapter 24, pp.398 - 399

[6] Younghusband, Sir Francis: *Kashmir*; as quoted by Mohamad, Khwaja Nazir, op.cit., Chapter 24, p.396

O.M. Burk visited Afghanistan in 1971-72 and wrote (as quoted by Hassnain and Olsson):

"The followers of Issa, son of Mariam, call themselves Muslims. Once a week, they join in a ritual meal in which bread and wine are taken as symbolic of grosser and finer nutrition, which are the experience of attainment of nearness to Allah. They are convinced too that the day would come when the world would discover the truth about Jesus".[7]

When Jesus became old and the time to leave the earth was approaching, he sent for his disciple *Yo-Bodh* to come. The disciple came and He gave all instructions about how his tomb should be built. The tomb was built on the place he died and it was called *Roza Bal* in Srinagar, known thereafter as the tomb of Jesus (Yusu Asaf). The tomb was constructed with dignity to show the greatness of the person buried within according to Jewish customs.

"First documentation is about circa AD 112, stating 'this is the tomb of Jesus, visited by kings and great people on pilgrimage here from all over the world".[8]

There are four important matters which were significant with respect to Roza Bal, the tomb of Jesus:

1. The walking stick (*rod*), which He always carried with Him, was laid near His tomb.
2. A wooden cross was put in front of the wooden coffin.
3. One stone slab with carved footprints showing the nail wounds on both feet.
4. The grave is laid east to west, according to the Jewish custom.

---

[7] Burk O M : *Among the Dervishes*; as quoted by Hassnain, Prof. Fida & Olsson, Suzanne, op.cit., Chapter 5, p. 104

[8] Hassnain, Prof. Fida & Olsson, Suzanne, op. cit., Chapter 6, p. 137

In AD 1443, Nasir-ud-din, a Muslim saint, was buried beside the grave of Jesus in Roza Bal.

Mir Saad-ullah Shahabadi, in his *Bagh-i-Sulaiman*, compiled in AD 1780, describes Roza Bal in these verses:

"The pious Naseeruddin, the spiritual guide of the virtuous; his tomb is in Khanyar, in the house at Anzimar. Within the tomb so famous is the Sepulcher of the Prophet, so illuminating! Whosoever bows before it receives inner light, solace, and contentment. Legends say that there was a prince, most accomplished, pious and great, who received the Kingdom of God. He was so faithful to the Lord that he was raised to the status of the Prophet. Through His grace he became the guide to the people of the Valley (of Kashmir). Here lies the sepulcher of that Prophet, who is known as Yuzu-Asaph."[9]

The present custodian of the tomb showed noted archaeologist Prof. Fida Hassnain a decree dated 1194 AH (AD 1766) granted by the Grand Mufti of Kashmir showing his right to the tomb:

> *The seal of the Justice of Islam, Mulla Fazil, 1194 in the High Court of Justice, the Department of Lear-ning and Piety of the Kingdom of Kashmir.*

Present: Rehman Khan, son of Amir Khan, submits that since ancient times many kings, nobles, ministers and the multitude visit this holy tomb of Yazu Asaph, the prophet of Allah, and make offerings in cash and kind.

Claim: "I claim that I am the only and absolute claimant, entitled to receive the offerings, and no one else has any right whatsoever on these offerings. I pray that a writ of injunction be granted and all others restrained from interfering with these rights".

---

[9] Mir Saad Ullah Shahabadi: *Bagh-i-Sulaiman;* as quoted by Hassnain, Prof. Fida & Olsson, Suzanne, op.cit., Chapter 6, p.139

Verdict: Now this High Court, after due consideration of the evidence, concludes as under:

It has been established that during the reign of Raja Gopadatta, who had built and repaired many temples, including the throne of Solomon on the Solomon Hill, Yuzu Asaph came to the valley of Kashmir. Prince by descent, he was pious and saintly and had given up earthly pursuits. He spent all his time in prayers and meditation.

The people of Kashmir, having become idolaters after the great flood of Noah, sent Yuzu Asaph as prophet for the people. This great prophet proclaimed the oneness of God. When he breathed his last, he was buried in this tomb, which is known [as] Rozabal. In the year 871 AH (1443 A.D.), Syed Nasir-ud-din, a descendant of Hazrat Imam Mosa Raza, was buried beside the grave of Yuzu Asaph.

Order: Since the shrine is visited by numerous devotees and since the applicant Rehman Khan is the hereditary custodian of this shrine, it is ordered that he is entitled to receive all offerings, and none else has any right to claim the offerings.

Given under our hand, 11th Jamad- Ulsant, 1194, signed and sealed: Mulla Fazil, Mohammad Azam, Faquir Baba, Abdul Shakoor, Mohammad Akbar, Raza Akbar Atta.[10]

According to the history of Kashmir, Yuzu Asaf passed away in AD 109. He was about 117 years old.

Why was the body of Muslim saint Naseeruddin buried near the grave of Jesus in Roza Bal? The obvious answer is that when the people living in

---

[10] Hassnain, Prof. Fida: *A Search for the Historical Jesus*, Gateway Books, UK 1994, Chapter 17, pp. 186 - 188

Kashmir embraced Islam, they wanted to downgrade the popularity of Yusu Asaf (Jesus). Prof. Fida Hassnain and Susanne Olson note:

> *"After being buried in Roza Bal next to Yuzu Asaf, Naseeruddin became the highly regarded saint inside the tomb, while Yusu Asaf became more and more a shadowy person of uncertain history who was being relegated further and further into the background of his own tomb, the Roza Bal. It is a strange twist of fate that the founder of the world's largest and most significant religion is now a second class occupant of his own burial chamber."[11]*

Something similar was done by the Hindus in Kashmir to the Temple of Solomon, which was built around BC 220.

The most ancient and historical building in Kashmir with the original name *Iyesht- eswara* was renamed *Takht-i-Sulaiman* (the throne of Solomon) after AD 78. This magnificent temple, atop the hill facing the Dal Lake, is dedicated to King Solomon and *"is an exact replica of the tomb of Absalom, the third son of David, in the woods of Ephraim, not far from Jerusalem, in the valley of Josephat."[12]*

> *"It is now called Shankaracharya [hill], but the Brahmins in the valley were unanimous in their belief that its original name was Iyesht-eswara. Its erection they ascribed to Jaloka, the son of Ashoka, who reigned about 220 B.C."[13]*

While the Muslims in Kashmir could be faulted for trying to downgrade and erase the heritage of Jesus for reasons of their changed faith, the Roman Church must take the responsibility for what it had done against Jesus with the dogma, namely, his *Ascension*. In order to justify the

---

[11] Hassnain, Prof. Fida & Olsson; op. cit., chapter 6, p. 122
[12] Mohamad, Khwaja Nazir: *Jesus in Heaven on Earth*, op.cit., Chapter 21, p. 346
[13] Cunningham ; as quoted by Hassnain, Prof. Fida & Olsson, Suzanne, op.cit., Chapter 5, p.109

dogma, the Roman Church lied, manipulated, distorted and destroyed all original documents concerning the life of Jesus and Thomas in Parthia as well as in Kashmir. Beginning from the third century until the end of the Second World War in Europe, the Roman Church made the life of millions of Jews miserable and inhuman under the Roman Empire and later in all European countries. The Jews were hounded and relegated to ghettos and separated from Christians. And the last Holocaust of the Jews in Europe was organized and conducted by a German Christian named Adolf Hitler with the silent acquiescence of the Roman Church.

But one day the truth about Jesus' life in Kashmir must come out.

In his famous book, *Jesus in Heaven on Earth*, Khwaja Nazir Ahamad wrote about two things he personally experienced during his research in Kashmir, namely, Jesus' walking stick and the stone of Moses.

A) The Holy *Rod*, the Companion of Jesus:

Jesus always carried a stick wherever he went.

> *"In case of epidemics and other disease, intercession services were held in all the mosques. The reputed stick of Christ, which is kept in Shah-i-Hamadan, was brought out. If an improper use is made of this reputed stick of Christ, it is said to bring floods".[14]*

In his book Khwaja Nazir Ahamad claims having seen this rod which he claims is still there in Kashmir. He writes:

> *"The last incident took place about 600 years ago. About a hundred years ago it was removed to Pakhil (Hazara Disrtict), but*

---

[14] Capt. C.M. Enrique: *the Realms of the gods;* ; as quoted by Mohamad, Khwaja Nazir, op.cit., Chapter 24, p. 397

was brought to Kashmir and deposited at the shrine of Hazarat Zain-ud-adin Wali in Aish Muqam. The rod is said to be that of Jesus (some attribute its origin to Moses) and is called Balagir. **I went to see this rod on 19ᵗʰ July 1947.** *With great difficulty we were permitted to see and photograph it. In fact we were allowed to see it only because we mentioned the drought then facing the valley, as a consequence of which the rice crop was likely to fail and famine set in. The rod is brownish - black in colour and is made of olive wood. It is 8 ft.3 in. in length and tapers from 1 ¾ inch to 1 ¼ inch in diameter. The ferrule of the rod is made of steel which is very old, but the top blade, like a spear-head, is comparatively new. Crooks must have broken off and the spear-head substituted. It is a fact that during April to July, 1947, there had hardly been any rain in the valley. There was very little water in the streams of the Jhelum river, and crops were being damaged for want of water. Incredible as it may seem, it is nevertheless a fact, that within half an hour of our seeing the rod rain began to pour down and it rained heavily for about an hour not only in Aish Muqam but throughout the valley".*[15]

B) The Stone of Moses:

Moses is a famous name for the Kashmir people since centuries. People believe that Moses retired to the Kashmir Valley *(Heaven on Earth)* from Palestine when he was old and he died and was buried in Kashmir.

Khwaja Nazir Ahamad claims to have visited the tomb of Moses in Kashmir and he wrote:

> *"The tomb itself is in a quadrangular enclosure and in it there are three other covered tombs. One of them is of Sang Bibi, the*

---

[15] Mohamad, Khwaja Nazir, op. ct. Chapter 24, p. 397

hermitess, and the other two are of her disciples. All these three tombs, like Muslim graves, are in the north-south direction. The fourth is the tomb of Moses, which, like the Jewish graves, is in the east-west direction".

"The tomb of Moses is on Nebu baal (Mount Nebu). From this place Behatpoor (Bandipur), Sin Betour (second Mount Sinai) are visible. Hashba, Pisgah and Maqam-i-Musa, the place of Moses, are within a short distance".[16]

There was a famous stone in a temple compound in the town *Bijibihara*, about 45 km from Srinagar, with the name *Sang -i-Musa* (the stone of Moses*)*. The Ladakhis call Moses 'Ka Ka'. Khwaja Nazir Ahamad got the opportunity to see the stone in 1947 and wrote what he experienced:

*"The stone of Moses is also mentioned in Rajatarangani. It weighs about 110 lbs. There is a tradition about this stone which **I tested myself.** We were told that, if eleven people sat around it and put one finger each beneath the stone and called out **Ka Ka, Ka Ka,** the stone would lift itself from the ground. I was accompanied by four other friends and we collected six local people and tried the experiment in the manner indicated. The stone rose to a height of four feet from the ground and we did not feel its weight at all. We tried it with ten and then with twelve persons. The stone did not move. We tried again with eleven and it kept on rising so long as we all were shouting **Ka Ka, Ka Ka.** This time we carried it shoulder high when one of us began to laugh and the stone fell to the ground. On questioning the significance of eleven persons we were told that out of twelve tribes of Israel one (Levi) had been disinherited. The remaining eleven tribes must be symbolically represented before the stone of Moses would move itself."[17]*

---

[16] Mohamad, Khwaja Nazir, ibid., Chapter 19, pp.280/ 283
[17] Mohamad, Khwaja Nazir, ibid., Chapter 19, pp.283-284

(The author visited the temple in Bijibihara in August 2015; but the stone Sang-i-Musa is no more in the temple compound)

Afghans and Kashmiris:

Afghanistan and Kashmir had received several people belonging to the *lost ten tribes* (Bani Israel) since about BC 500. They lived as Jews keeping their old Jewish traditions. Jesus returned to Kashmir seeking those *lost ten tribes*.

According to Mir Alam Nashbandi, the tribal head in Gutlipora, 30 km north of Srinagar, they are descendants of Jacob of Israel which is why they are called Bani Israel.

"We became Muslims many centuries ago and before our conversion we were Buddhists. Before that, we were Bani Israel. We were destined to suffer and scatter all over the world and we came to Kashmir via Gilgit and Chitral, leaving some of our brethren behind in Iran, Turkey, Samarkand and Afghanistan".[18]

Sir Alexander Burns in his book *Travels into Bokhara, published in 1835, wrote:*

*".....they say that they lived as Jews till Khalid summoned them **in the first century of the Mohammadans** to assist in the war against the infidels. For their services on that occasion Kayse, their leader, got the title Abdool- rasheed, which means the son of the mighty. He was also told to consider himself as the Butan, Arabic for mast of the tribe, on which their posterity would hinge..... Since that time the Afghans are sometimes*

---

[18] Khayal, Gulam Nabi: *India Today*, March 31, 1982

called **Putan** (or **Pathan**) by which name they are familiarly known in India".[19]

The people belonging to the lost ten tribes who lived in Afghanistan and Kashmir accepted Islam. Now the majority of them are Muslims, but they still maintain many of their old Jewish traditions.

In Kashmir there is a group of people called Kashmiri Pandits who were of Jewish origin and belonged to *Bani Israel*, but later accepted Hinduism. Their social status in the society is equal to the Brahmins. And the Kashmiri Pundits continue to uphold certain old Jewish traditions.

There are many similarities in the customs followed by the Jews, the Afghans as well as Kashmir Muslims and Kashmiri Pandits. Some of them are given below:

1. Israelites: Fishes without fins and scales are forbidden.

- Afghans and Kashmiris : Afghans neither eat eels(which they call marmahi) nor another variety of fish named katasaraor nai - that is fishes without fins and scales. The Kashmiris do not eat eels. The Kashmiri Pandits will not eat ram gad, a small fish without fins or scale, but they, when questioned, cannot explain their aversion to this type of fish.

2. Israelites: Jews do not eat the sinews of the hollow to the thigh near the joint.

- Afghans and Kashmiris are most particular in removing them before cooking

3. Israelites: The flesh of swine is forbidden.

- Afghans and Kashmiris: The Holy Quran also forbids this. But Syed Jalalud Din Afghani rcords that Afghans did not eat the flesh of

---

[19] Sir Alexander Burns : *Travels into Bokhara;* as quoted by Mohamad, Khwaja Nazir, op. ct., Chapter 21, p. 299

swine even before their conversion to Islam. Kashmiri Pandits also do not eat the flesh of swine.

4. The tribes of Israel, though they had 'heads of tribes' and 'fathers of families', were tribal and not personal in their attachment and loyalty.

   - Afghans and Kashmiris: The attachment of Afghans in particular is tribal. The interests of the tribe are so completely paramount that the private wish of the Khan, the head of the tribe, is utterly disregarded if it is at variance with the honour or advantage of the tribe.

5. Israelites: Among the Jews, the laws of kinship demanded avenging the murder of a member of the family with murder. The law of retribution as laid down by Moses was "Life shall go for life, eye for eye, tooth for tooth, hand for hand, foot for foot".

- Afghans and Kashmiris are most revengeful. They very rarely forgive a wrong done to them, and never forget it. Among the Afghans the measure of 'life for a life...' is rigidly enforced.

6. The Kashmiri Pandits, though very conservative Hindus, do not treat Kashmiri Muslims as untouchables. They invariably employ Kashmiri Muslim women as wet-nurses for their children. It is significant that Kashmiri Pandits do not eat with or take their meal from the Brahmins of India. Kashmir Muslims and Pandits visit and venerate the same holy places in Kashmir. These peculiar features cannot be explained except on the ground of their common origin.

7. Both Afghans and Kashmiris claim to be Bani Israel *(children of Israel), but they consider the term Yahood (Jew) to be one of reproach. They hate Jews with the traditional hatred which Israel bore towards the tribe of Judah.*[20]

---

[20] Mohamad, Khwaja Nazir, op. ct., Chapter 21, pp.324 -344

Chapter 10

Conclusion

Such is the true story of Jesus Christ. Now we know the missing part in the Bible about Jesus' life between the age of 13 and 29 and His life after crucifixion. He belonged to India because He spent most part of His life in India. He is the most travelled person in the world for preaching His new faith. Many of His words (or similar ones) can be seen in Buddhism and Hinduism. For many Hindus, Jesus and Krishna are *avatars* (incarnation of God) in different times. Many believe that *"Christ was a Yogi who spent his early youth and life after crucifixion in India. He was a disciple of some great yogis of India.*[21]

The Quran, too, has several passages referring to Jesus and His mother with deep respect. Therefore, Jesus truly belongs not only to Christianity but also to all other religions in the world, where He has so many followers.

For an Indian spiritual Yogi, Jesus Christ is the Son of God. He has no problem following Jesus for his salvation. But, spiritually inclined Hindus and Thomas Christians would find it difficult to follow the Roman and other European Churches.

The teachings of Jesus as propagated by the Church are noble and universal. But His followers in Europe, namely, the Popes and the Church hierarchy and the kings and emperors, never really practised and followed His words until the French Revolution (1789-1799). His name was used only for propaganda. In the Middle Ages in Europe many innocent Christian men and women lost their lives in the *inquisition* and *witch-hunt*

---

[21] Sharma, Ram Murti: *Encyclopaedia of Vedanda;* as quoted by Bharat, Shady: *Christ Across the Ganges,* O Books, UK 2007, Chapter 4, p. 77

practised by the Church. During the European colonization of Asia, Africa and the Americas between the 15th and 20th century, the colonial powers made the life of indigenous people unbearable. The Church used force and inducements to convert people to Christianity which Jesus would never have accepted. It was only after the French Revolution that the European countries gradually accepted democracy, setting a demarcation line between Church and Government. The Church lost power and ceased to have influence and representation in governments. People elected their representatives to oversee administration. But the society as a whole and the elected representatives remained Christian, upholding the same values preached and followed by the Church since centuries. Governments followed the same aggressive policies and the consequence was the two World Wars in Europe in the twentieth century. Jesus preached *non-violence*, but the elected Christian governments were *violent* but claiming to follow Jesus Christ.

Consequently, for an ordinary Hindu, Jesus Christ has an aggressive face.

A normal Hindu is inspired when he reads the Bible because he comes across many principles and truths existing in Hinduism and Buddhism. For a true Hindu, Jesus is Son of God, an *avatar*. He is pious and the redeemer. A Hindu who believes in true Hinduism is not a religious fanatic. He will meditate on the teachings of Jesus Christ to free his soul and see within him *the Kingdom of God*. He wants to attain God while he lives on earth and not after death. What the European colonial countries and the Church did in the colonies was beyond his imagination. The Hindu was naturally suspicious and astonished at how the Christians could commit such atrocities on other human beings while professing to follow the teachings of Jesus Christ.

For the spiritually awakened Hindu, Jesus Christ has a smiling face, is peace-loving and non-violent.

Indeed, the correct *interpreters* of Jesus' words, for the understanding of the common man, have been the Hindu yogis of India like Ramakrishna Paramahans, Vivekananda, Swami Sivananda, Swami Yukteswar Giri of Puri and his famous disciple Paramahansa Yogananda, the founder of Self-Realization Fellowship of Los Angeles, California.

Jesus said: *"The Kingdom of God is within you"*. He taught His twelve disciples *the way* to reach *God within you* through meditation (*yoga*). He also taught that one has to attain God when one is living on earth. But His *official* followers lost the precious *way (yoga)* and they even teach that God is dwelling *in heaven* and one can attain Him *only after death*.

We need in the world a true Christianity following the path of Jesus Christ respecting and tolerant of all other religions. As Mahatma Gandhi said, *"Be a better Christian"* and there is no need for a Christian to be converted to Hinduism or a Hindu to be converted to Christianity. This is valid for all religions because there is only one God.

People are more attracted to materialism than to human morals, though they visit at least once a week a church or temple or mosque. In today's world, one has no problem with one's conscience to amass great wealth by hook or by crook and shutting the eyes to children, women and men living in utter poverty in the neighbourhood. The world was never so rich as it is today, but the people in many countries of the world are so poor as never before. Only a part of the mankind gets to enjoy the fruits of the whole world. It is wrong.

Injustice can't be justified again by injustice, but ONLY by justice.

The richness of the world belongs to the people of the world irrespective of which country or which religion one is born in. Mankind has forgotten the teachings of Krishna, the Buddha, Jesus Christ, Mohammad and Shankaracharya. Materialism has become the new god of mankind. We have to go back to the roots of their teachings in order to achieve a peaceful and harmonious world where each human being is respected and accepted as a *human being* irrespective of his nationality, race or colour.

Because they are all *children of God.*

The Roza Bal Shrine of Jesus Christ in Srinagar, Kashmir, belongs to all religious people because His words are universal and He has followers in all religions. Anybody who wishes to visit the shrine should have the right to visit Him. Muslims are the present custodians of the Roza Bal Shrine and all religious people in the world should be thankful to them for respectfully maintaining and protecting the Shrine since the death of Jesus Christ. As proposed by Prof. Fida Hassnain of Kashmir, the Roza Bal Shrine in Srinagar should be put under the legal authority of UNESCO World Heritage Site and controlled and supervised by the Government of India.

Photos

Tomb of Jesus, Khaniyar in Srinagar
Photo: M. Payoly, August 2015

Old Buddhist Monastery on a hill in Aish Muqam, where Jesus stayed first
when He came to Kashmir. Now it is a Mosque
Photo: M. Payoly, August 2015

Tomb of Moses, now covered by grass, near to the tree at Mount Nebu in Kashmir
Photo: M. Payoly, August 2015

Famous Buddhist Monastery in Hemis, near Leh in Ladakh
Photo: M. Payoly, August 2015

Pahalgam, beautiful valley of Marjan – Jesus` wife
Photo: M. Payoly, August 2015

Another beautiful view of Pahalgam
Photo: M. Payoly, August 2015

Yusu Marg, through the way Jesus first entered Kashmir and is named after Him

Photo: M. Payoly, August 2015

Prof. Fida M. Hassnain MA, LLB, D. Arch. D. Indol

Mr. Nicolas Notovitch

Zeitfracht Medien GmbH
Ferdinand-Jühlke-Straße 7
99095 Erfurt, Deutschland
produktsicherheit@kolibri360.de